500

baby & toddler foods

500

baby & toddler foods

Beverley Glock

APPLE

A Quintet Book

First published in the UK in 2011 by
Apple Press
7 Greenland Street
London NW1 0ND
United Kingdom

www.apple-press.com

ISBN: 978-1-84543-415-1
QTT.BTFO

This book was conceived, designed and produced by
Quintet Publishing Limited
6 Blundell Street
London N7 9BH
United Kingdom

Food Stylist: Nikki Gee
Photographer: Ian Garlick
Art Director: Michael Charles
Editorial Assistants: Sarah Quinlan, Holly Willsher
Project Editor: Anya Hayes
Managing Editor: Donna Gregory
Publisher: Mark Searle

10 9 8 7 6 5 4 3 2

Printed in China by 1010 Printing International Ltd.

contents

introduction

Weaning a baby can be daunting, especially for a new parent. When should you start feeding solids? Which foods should you give your baby? Which foods should you avoid? How much should you give? What texture should the food be? The questions go on and on, and you suddenly realise that breast or bottle feeding is actually very easy.

This book will help answer those questions while inspiring you with simple, nutritious recipes for babies from their very first foods right through the toddler years. By making your own baby food, you'll save money and you'll know exactly what you're feeding your child, not worrying about checking ingredients on commercial baby food labels. Most of the recipes in this book are designed for the whole family to eat, so everyone eats the same meal, making your life easier.

ages & stages for solid foods

It's very important to introduce solid foods to your baby gradually and at the right time in their development. So read this section carefully and talk to your doctor if you have any questions. Also, read the section on food allergies and foods to restrict (pages 12–19) as well as the information on the 'four-day rule' on page 8.

NEVER leave babies or toddlers on their own when they are eating. It is easy for them to choke on food or put it in inappropriate places such as ears and noses, so make sure that a responsible adult is always with them.

baby's first foods (4-6 months)

Do not give solid food to babies under 4 months, as their digestion is not ready and they should be wholly fed on breast milk or formula.

The recommended age to begin weaning is around 4-6 months; each baby is different and some are ready for solid food earlier than others. You need to trust your instincts and watch for signs from your baby that he or she is ready for some solid food. If your baby has been sleeping through the night and then starts waking up during the night demanding food, or begins drinking more breast milk or formula and does not seem satisfied, it may be time to introduce a little solid food. Always check with your doctor first.

Other signs of readiness to look for are:

• good head control

• trunk stability, able to sit alone in a high chair

• starts to reach for your food

• ability to swallow foods without gagging

Even when you've introduced some solid food, breast milk or formula should still be the primary food you give your baby.

Begin with one teaspoonful, once a day, of a solid food, usually rice cereal mixed with breast milk or formula, which is easy to digest. Once your baby has successfully eaten this for four or five days, with no adverse reaction, you can introduce a single fruit or vegetable. Wait for four days before introducing another. This is called the 'four-day rule'. By introducing one new food at a time, you can determine if your baby has an intolerance or allergic reaction to that food. Once you know which foods your baby enjoys and can safely eat, you can keep feeding them to your baby as well as trying new ones too. Work up to an ice cube-size (or 25 g/1 oz), which is a portion for a young baby.

The food should be very puréed and have a sloppy, liquid consistency. If needed, add breast milk, formula or the cooking liquid to the purée to achieve this very thin consistency. Young babies may have problems eating thick purées and may gag on them.

moving forward (6–9 months)

At this stage, babies can now eat virtually the same food as the rest of the family, but without any salt and more mashed than food for the adults. Gradually begin to introduce new flavours by using small amounts of herbs and spices. Make sure you check that all the ingredients are recommended for the age of your baby and omit any from the adult meal that are not suitable. Your baby will grow up knowing that children and adults eat the same food and everyone eats together. This goes a long way to prevent fussy eaters.

You'll still purée or mash the food, but it'll be a thicker purée than before. Keep portions based on 1 cube (25 g/1 oz), but now introduce solids to more than 1 meal per day. If the recipes calls for, say, one banana, a 6-month-old baby cannot eat a whole banana, but he or she would eat up to ¼ mashed. The rest of the purée can be refrigerated or frozen.

Breast milk or formula should still be the baby's main drink up to the age of 12 months. You may give fruit juices in very small amounts – no more than ¼ cup for babies under the age of 12 months. Juices must be 100 per cent pasteurized fruit or vegetable juice, definitely not a fruit drink or juice drink. Juice should always be given from a cup, and not from a bottle. A bottle keeps the juice in contact with the baby's teeth for longer and can cause cavities.

At this stage, you can introduce dairy products such as yoghurt, cream cheese, crème fraîche and pasteurized cheese. These should be full-fat dairy products, because children under the age of 2 years need a diet that is 40–50 per cent fat. However, do not give babies under 12 months cow's milk as a beverage or even in cooking (see page 14.)

Eggs can be introduced if they are thoroughly cooked; scrambled eggs and omelettes are good. Meat, chicken, turkey and fish can be added at this stage. Start with milder flavours, such as chicken and white fish, before introducing beef, lamb or salmon, so your baby has time to get used to new textures and flavours, before gradually adding stronger flavoured food. Always mash the meat or fish first and offer separately from a vegetable or mixed together, depending on your baby's preference. Add liquid to make it easier to swallow.

baby-led weaning

When your baby is 6 months and older, you could consider baby-led weaning, which means moving straight to finger food and allowing babies to feed themselves. No puréeing, no mashing, no tiny baby spoons. Whether you go this route depends on when you wean your baby, as baby-led weaning is not suitable for babies under 6 months old. It also depends on you as a parent and whether you prefer the traditional method of puréeing and mashing the food your 6-month-old eats.

My personal preference is the traditional method combined with the introduction of some soft finger foods. The World Health Organization suggests that babies should be fed puréed food at the beginning of weaning as well as being given some finger foods. Baby-led weaning can be very messy: food ends up on the floor, there can be a lot of waste and it is quite difficult to determine exactly how much food your baby has eaten.

If you choose to follow baby-led weaning solely, you will have to make sure that the food you give your baby is not too slippery to hold, as they will have difficulty and become frustrated. This could lead to fussy eating. So grind up oat-based breakfast cereal or rolled oats to a powder and use it to coat tofu, mango slices or any other food that is difficult to hold. Also, the food should be soft and chunky, as babies don't develop a pincer grip until after 6 months and will need to hold their food in their fist. Foods like broccoli florets and toast fingers are ideal.

eating with the family (9–12 months)
By now, babies are starting to assert their independence, holding forks and spoons and feeding themselves, although a lot of food will miss their mouths. Milk teeth may be coming through, making it easier for babies to bite. It's time to introduce textures and different

colours, so don't purée their food quite as much. Still, be very careful to give them nothing they can choke on. Stay clear of whole grapes, whole berries, cubes of hard fruit and vegetables and other hard food until children are over 3 years of age, as they are a perfect shape and size for children to choke on. You can, however, cut foods into very small pieces so babies can handle them better, and they won't become lodged in their windpipe.

toddlers (12 months & up)
Regularly introduce your toddler to new foods and new flavours. Take toddlers to the supermarket and let them choose a different fruit or vegetable to try each week. They'll feel they have more control over their food. Food doesn't need to be bland; in fact, the younger you introduce children to new flavours, the less fussy they'll be as they get older.

As soon as toddlers show an interest in cooking, let them help. If they can stand unaided and hold a spoon, they can participate in the kitchen. Toddlers enjoy stirring — even if they just have their own bowl and copy you when you're stirring — and they enjoy using their fingers to help you 'rub in' the fat and flour to make gingerbread, biscuits and thumbprint cookies. You'll be introducing them to a skill that will last a lifetime — cooking.

Watch out for how much sugar they eat (toddlers will love everything sugary!) and keep their juice intake to no more than 50–100 g (2–4 oz) a day of 100 per cent juices, not juice drinks. Milk is still the best drink for toddlers, and it can now be cow's milk.

food restrictions

For various reasons, some foods are unsuitable for babies of certain ages. They fall into the category of 'forbidden foods' or 'restricted foods'.

Remember, it's always advisable to check with your doctor before starting your baby on solid food. Also, if there is any family history of food allergies or intolerances, it is definitely best to consult your doctor regularly while introducing new foods to your baby.

Always remember the four-day rule when trying out new foods. That is, introduce them one at a time and wait for four days to see if there has been any reaction before you introduce another new food. This will help you determine if your baby has any allergies or intolerances to individual foods.

What is the difference between a food allergy and a food intolerance? An allergy is when the body mistakes a food for a dangerous invader and tries to expel it. To do this, the body produces antibodies, which in turn release chemicals called histamines. When histamines are released, the body produces symptoms such as runny nose, itchy eyes, redness around the mouth and rashes (similar symptoms to hay fever, which is an allergic reaction to pollen).

Very occasionally an anaphylactic reaction can occur, which is potentially life-threatening. If this happens, call for an ambulance immediately to go straight to the hospital.

Anaphylactic symptoms are:

- breathing problems
- severe swelling of the face, lips and throat
- increased heart rate/racing pulse
- sweating
- fainting
- ultimately death if not treated quickly

A food intolerance is not life-threatening but can be highly unpleasant. Symptoms are usually associated with the stomach, such as vomiting and diarrhoea, stomach cramps or a headache or rash.

foods that can cause food allergies

There are eight food substances that cause most food allergies. Even the tiniest exposure to a specific food can cause children and adults who are allergic to suffer reactions, whether they have consumed it themselves or not. It even could be that someone is eating peanuts when someone with a peanut allergy walks into the same room. The eight foods are:

- dairy
- eggs
- peanuts
- shellfish
- gluten (usually from wheat)
- tree nuts (such as cashews, walnuts, pecans)
- soya
- fish

dairy products

Dairy products are made from cow's milk and include yoghurt, cheese, cream, crème fraîche and butter. Babies under 6 months old should not be given any dairy products. Cow's milk should not be used as a drink for babies until they are at least 12 months old, nor should cow's milk itself be used in cooking for babies under 12 months.

Cow's milk hinders iron absorption. Iron is critical to support the growth of a human baby. Also, cow's milk can be difficult for babies to digest. Other dairy products such as yoghurt and cheese are cultured and are easier on young digestive systems. This is why it is fine to give babies 6 months and older dairy products, but not cow's milk until they are 12 months. Do not give babies or toddlers unpasteurized cheese, milk or other dairy products, goat's or sheep's cheese, or mould-ripened cheese, because of the risk of listeria.

gluten & wheat

Gluten is a protein found in wheat and other grains, such as barley, and can be a cause of allergy and intolerance. Oats do not contain gluten, but may be contaminated with it during the manufacturing process, so to be cautious you should introduce oats no earlier than 6 months old, and if there is no adverse reaction, you can move on to wheat. Wheat is a common cause of allergy and intolerance, so introduce to your baby after 9 months old. Wheat or gluten intolerance (coeliac disease) is often a lifelong condition that will mean total restriction of consuming anything with wheat or gluten. Please consult your doctor about this issue.

eggs

Eggs are a good source of protein and iron; however, they must be thoroughly cooked. Eggs can contain salmonella, a source of food poisoning. Avoid foods using unpasteurized raw egg, such as homemade mayonnaise, mousses and ice cream, and do not allow your baby to lick the spoon if you have been making cake batter. Commercial mayonnaise and ice creams are generally pasteurized, but always check the label before offering to a young child. When your baby is 6 months or older, you can introduce eggs in a small amount, as some babies are highly allergic to eggs. (This is uncommon, but it's best to be safe.)

soya

Soya is a legume, part of the pea and bean family, as are peanuts. (If children and adults are allergic to soya beans and soya products, they might be able to eat other legumes with no reaction.) Avoid edamame beans, soy sauce, miso, soya beans, tofu, textured vegetable protein (TVP), tamari and tempeh. Soya protein is a common food additive that can be included in soups, stock, starches, medicines, flavourings and colourings, so read the labels carefully.

peanuts

Peanut allergy is becoming more common, and many children and adults who are allergic to peanuts and peanut oil are also allergic to tree nuts. People with severe nut allergies may react to only very small, or trace, amounts of nuts.

tree nuts

These are nuts that grow on trees, such as cashews, pecans, walnuts and almonds. Pine nuts also fall into this category, although they are not strictly a nut but a seed. If your child is allergic to peanuts, it is highly likely that they may also be allergic to tree nuts. Be careful when buying pesto, in case nuts other than pine nuts have been included, and also read the labels of body lotion, shampoo, suntan lotion and other toiletries, as tree nut oil is frequently used as an ingredient. They do not have to be ingested to cause a reaction; just touching an allergen can start a reaction for someone who is severely allergic.

fish & shellfish

Start your baby on white fish such as flounder beginning at 6 months, and move them on to salmon and other oily fish if they show no reaction to the white fish. But do not give babies or toddlers swordfish, because this carries a high risk of mercury in their flesh. Also be very cautious of mackerel, tuna, halibut, sea trout and sea bass because they contain some mercury. Give them only in moderation. If in any doubt, consult your doctor. Providing there is no history of shellfish allergy in your family, shellfish should be fine to introduce to babies over 12 months old. Just be sure that the shellfish is from a reliable source and that it is well cooked.

other foods to restrict

The following foods may cause an adverse reaction with your baby, so introduce gradually, and monitor your baby carefully. With any adverse reaction, reintroduce after 12 months.

citrus & other acidic fruit

Tomatoes, kiwi fruit and pineapples can be acidic, so introduce gradually after 6 months and watch your baby's reaction carefully. Some babies love them and have no problems, others have an adverse reaction which means you should hold off and reintroduce after 12 months. Citrus fruit tends to be acidic and can possibly lead to an upset tummy in young babies. It's best to introduce any citrus (including oranges, lemons, limes, grapefruit and clementines) gradually after 9 months, and montor their reaction.

strawberries & other berries
Strawberries are a common allergen, so it is advisable not to introduce them until baby is over 12 months old. Raspberries and blackberries are slightly acidic and can cause an upset tummy, so it may be suitable to wait until your baby is 12 months old.

honey, maple syrup & corn syrup
Never give a baby under 12 months old honey, maple syrup or corn syrup. These products may contain the bacteria *Clostridium botulinum*, which produces toxins in a baby's intestines leading to infant botulism. Once babies are over a year old, their intestines have matured sufficiently to prevent this bacteria from growing.

sugary foods
Do not feed your baby sugary foods, such as cakes, biscuits and chocolate, before 12 months. Babies do not need these foods, and the longer they are kept away from them the more likely they will try — and like — fresh fruit and vegetables and other more healthy options.

salt
We add salt to our food to make it taste better, but babies will accept food for how it tastes without salt (as we adults would if we had never tried it). Salt is dangerous to babies. It can lead to high blood pressure and possible kidney failure.

equipment for making baby food

There's nothing specific that you must have for making baby food, but the following items — which are common in most kitchens — are very helpful.

digital weighing scales, measuring cups & spoons
These make your life easy by ensuring that the quantities are correct, especially when baking muffins and bread. Small measuring cups are especially helpful for making the small quantities needed for babies.

blenders & food processors
When you're puréeing a small amount of food, a handheld blender is your best bet. They also are useful for puréeing soups directly in the saucepan. Blenders and food processors are good for bigger quantities such as for making smoothies, and they can be used to make breadcrumbs, purée hummus, and prepare other dips.

potato masher, potato ricer & food mill
A handheld potato masher will make quick work of mashing a pan of boiled potatoes, as well as any cooked root vegtables or stewed fruits. Potato ricers give a much finer and smoother texture and also are good for preparing baby food. A food mill is a stainless steel utensil that grinds meat, poultry, fish, vegetables and fruit to a purée.

standing mixers & mixing bowls

Heavy-duty electric mixers make short work of mixing pizza and bread dough, pancakes and muffins, and beating eggs. Some models come with a wide range of attachments to help you make your own pasta dough and minced meat. Lightweight stainless steel bowls that are dishwasher-proof and unbreakable are a sound investment, especially when your toddler starts to help you cook.

chopping boards

Keep one chopping board purely for raw meat to prevent cross-contamination and make sure that it is washed thoroughly after use. A second chopping board can be used for fruits and vegetables, cooked meats and other items you need to chop. A non-stick plastic board suitable for dishwashers is ideal. Avoid glass chopping boards, as they will blunt your knives and tend to be slippery to work with.

oventop cookware & ovenware

Solid stainless steel saucepans in different sizes are invaluable. A steamer basket (which you set over a pan of boiling water) is good for cooking vegetables, because they are more nutritious steamed than boiled. A non-stick frying pan is good for reducing the amount of oil and fat you cook with, making food healthier for baby and the rest of the family. Baking tins and muffin tins should be non-stick. Look for good-quality, solid tins. It is worth paying a little more, knowing that they will last you a long time.

parchment paper & clingfilm
Use parchment paper to line baking tins and to roll pastry and biscuit and bread dough on. You will not need to use as much flour on the work surface, so there is much less cleaning to do. Clingfilm is essential to cover food to be kept in the refrigerator.

timers
When you have a baby or toddler, you will need a kitchen timer to remind you of foods you have cooking. It is difficult to remember everything when you are distracted by children.

ice cube trays, freezer containers & bags
When starting to make baby food, you'll find ice cube trays are ideal for freezing purées. Each cube is a 25 g (1 oz) serving. The recipes in this book provide more than one serving, so you can freeze cubes for meals for the next few weeks, or you could even enlist the help of family or friends to help you out in the first few months of life with a baby! After the cubes are frozen, transfer them to a freezer-weight plastic bag, label the bag with the name of the food and the date, and replace in the freezer.

As your baby grows, you will need bigger containers. Freezer containers with lids come in different sizes and are ideal for freezing individual meal portions. Always label the container with the name of the food and the date it was made, and use the oldest food first.

baby food safety techniques

Food safety and personal hygiene must be especially stringent when preparing baby food.

- Do not handle food with unwashed hands, and wash your hands thoroughly after handling raw meat, poultry and fish. Keep utensils and boards very clean.

- Freshly cooked food must be cooled quickly, within 90 minutes, and then placed in a sealed container in the refrigerator. If it is to be frozen, transfer the freshly made food to an ice cube tray (if making 25 g/1 oz servings) or single-serving freezer containers with lids, and cool quickly before placing in the freezer. To cool food quickly, place the ice cube tray or freezer container in an ice bath or cold water in the sink.

- Be sure that raw meat and fish are stored at the bottom of the refrigerator or freezer to avoid cross-contamination with ready-to-eat food.

- Never put hot or warm food in the refrigerator or freezer, because the food will raise the temperature of the rest of the food inside. This could lead to bacteria breeding, which could cause food poisoning.

- Thoroughly defrost food before reheating, and only reheat once. The safest way to defrost is in the refrigerator overnight, or in the microwave. Do not defrost food under hot water or by leaving it on the counter, because bacteria will be able to multiply to unsafe levels.

- When feeding your baby, transfer the food in small amounts to a dish so you can add more with a clean spoon if baby is enjoying it. Do not feed your baby directly out of the container, because the spoon baby has eaten from could contaminate the food in the container.

- You can use your microwave for cooking and reheating: please follow the manufacturer's instructions. Microwave instructions are not included within the recipes due to varying power settings. If you are using a microwave, always ensure food is piping hot before serving.

- Always, always have a responsible adult supervise your baby's mealtimes and snacktimes.

baby's first foods

It's an exciting time when your baby is ready to start eating solid foods. All foods should be puréed and have a sloppy, liquid consistency. If needed, add breast milk, formula or the cooking liquid to the purée to achieve this very thin consistency. Have fun with it!

baby porridge

see variations page 43

Porridge for infants is made by grinding uncooked rice, never oats. Oats should not be given to babies before they are 6 months old, because oats may contain a small amount of gluten, a potential allergen.

600 g (21 oz) brown rice
scant 225 ml (8 fl. oz) cup water
breast milk or infant formula

Grind the rice in a blender, food processor or clean coffee/spice grinder until it becomes a very, very fine powder. Store in an airtight container and keep in a cool, dry place for up to 3 months.

To cook one portion, place the water in a small pan and bring to the boil. Add 50 g (2 oz) ground rice powder and simmer, stirring constantly, for 10 minutes. Remove from the heat and stir in enough breast milk or formula to achieve the desired consistency. Cool quickly and refrigerate within 30 minutes if you wish to keep some for another meal.

Use within 24 hours. Cooled porridge can be frozen immediately. Place in a freezerproof container, label and freeze for up to 1 month. To use from frozen, defrost thoroughly and heat through fully, then serve.

Makes 8–12 portions

melon purée

see variations page 44

Ripe melon — cantaloupe, Galia, or honeydew — is easy to mash for babies. It has a mild flavour and complements other fruit well. Melon is high in water content, so you may not need extra liquid when it is puréed.

1 whole melon
275–375 ml (10–14 fl. oz) breast milk
or formula

Slice and peel the melon, and chop the flesh into chunks. Mash with a fork or purée in a blender or food processor, adding breast milk or formula until it is a semi-liquid consistency. Serve 3–4 tablespoons per portion for young babies.

You can either cover and refrigerate for up to 48 hours, or freeze in ice cube trays until solid, then transfer to a freezer bag, label and use within 1 month. To defrost, simply remove 2 or 3 cubes of frozen melon purée, allow to come to room temperature, stir and serve.

Makes 20–24 portions

apple purée

see variations page 45

Apples such as Braeburn, Gala, Golden Delicious and Fuji work well in this recipe.

8 apples
150–225 ml (5–8 fl. oz) breast milk or formula

Peel, core and chop or slice the apples. Place the apple pieces in a saucepan with enough water to just cover them, then boil or steam until the apple pieces are tender. Drain (and reserve) any excess water, then mash or purée the apples with a little breast milk, formula or the cooking water until the purée has the required consistency.

You can cover and refrigerate the puréed apple for 24 hours. Alternatively, freeze in ice cube trays until solid, then transfer to a freezer bag, label and use within 1 month. To defrost, simply remove 2 or 3 cubes of frozen apple purée, allow to come to room temperature, stir, and serve.

Makes 30 portions

banana purée

see variations page 46

Bananas are almost the perfect food. Fresh, they are easily carried in a bag, giving you an instant baby meal. All you need is a fork to mash the banana with. Choose ripe bananas as they are easier to mash than unripe bananas. Also, babies can have difficulty digesting unripe bananas.

4 ripe bananas, peeled
3–4 tbsp breast milk or formula

Mash or purée the flesh of the bananas with a little breast milk or formula until it has the desired consistency.

You can refrigerate the mashed banana for 24 hours, but it tends to go brown quickly. Freeze mashed bananas in ice cube trays until solid, then transfer to a freezer bag, label and use within 1 month. To defrost, simply remove 2 or 3 cubes of frozen banana purée, allow to come to room temperature, stir and serve.

Makes 4–8 portions

mashed sweet potato

see variations page 47

Sweet potatoes mash easily, are easy to digest and naturally sweet, and make an ideal first food for babies. You can bake or steam the potato.

2 sweet potatoes
2–4 tbsp breast milk or formula

To bake: Preheat the oven to 220°C (425°F/Gas mark 7). Wash the sweet potatoes and prick all over with a fork to prevent it from bursting while it is cooking. Wrap the potates in kitchen foil and place onto a small baking tin to stop any sticky juices from dripping into the oven. Bake for 30–60 minutes until soft. Remove from the oven, discard the foil and leave to cool. Slit the potatoes lengthwise, scoop out the flesh and discard the skin.

To steam: Wash and peel the potatoes and chop into cubes. Place the potato cubes in a colander set over a saucepan of boiling water, cover with a lid, and steam for 10–15 minutes until tender.

Mash or purée the baked or steamed potato flesh with a little breast milk or formula.

You can either cover and refrigerate for up to 48 hours, or freeze in ice cube trays until solid, then transfer to a freezer bag, label and use within 1 month. To defrost, simply remove 2 or 3 cubes of frozen mashed sweet potato, allow to come to room temperature, stir, heat through fully and serve.

Makes 10–12 portions

mashed potato

see variations page 48

Potatoes are high in fibre and a great vegetable to introduce to babies early in their weaning. By adding brightly coloured vegetables to the potato, you introduce different flavours and textures, and suddenly a plain old potato becomes much more exciting. Always introduce new foods one at a time, a few days apart.

2 potatoes
2–4 tbsp breast milk or formula

To bake: Preheat the oven to 220°C (425°F/Gas mark 7). Wash the potatoes and prick all over with a fork to prevent from bursting while cooking. Wrap in kitchen foil and bake on the top shelf of your oven for 50-60 minutes, until soft. Remove, discard the foil and leave to cool. Slit the potatoes lengthwise, scoop out the flesh and discard the skins.

To steam or boil: Wash and peel the potatoes, chop into cubes. If steaming, place in a steamer over a pan of boiling water and cook for 20–25 minutes, until tender. If boiling, bring a pan of water to a boil, add the potatoes, and simmer for 15–20 minutes, until soft.

Mash or purée the cooked potatoes with a little breast milk or formula. Serve or cover and refrigerate for up to 48 hours. Alternatively, freeze in ice cube trays until solid, then transfer to a freezer bag, label and use within 1 month. To defrost, remove 2 or 3 cubes, allow to come to room temperature, stir, heat through fully and serve.

Makes 10–12 portions

mashed butternut squash

see variations page 49

Butternut squash freezes really well. A whole squash will fill up a whole ice cube tray and give you extra to make a family meal. It is a very versatile vegetable, and delicious roasted.

1 small butternut squash
1 tbsp mild olive oil
2–4 tbsp breast milk or formula

To roast: Preheat the oven to 220°C (425°F/Gas mark 7). Halve the butternut squash and scoop out the seeds. Cut the halves into slices, brush with a little olive oil and roast for 20–30 minutes, until soft. Remove from the oven, set aside to cool slightly, then peel. Purée or mash with a little breast milk or formula.

To steam: Halve the butternut squash, scoop out the seeds, then peel and chop into 2-cm (¾-in) cubes. Steam over boiling water for 15–20 minutes until tender. Mash or purée the flesh with a little breast milk or formula, and serve. Leave the breast milk out of the portions for the whole family.

You can either cover and refrigerate for up to 48 hours, or freeze in ice cube trays until solid, then transfer to a freezer bag, label, and use within 1 month. To defrost, simply remove 2 or 3 cubes of frozen mashed butternut squash, allow to come to room temperature, stir, heat through fully and serve.

Makes 8–10 portions

swede & apple purée

see variations page 50

Swede has a strong flavour, which makes it a good first food because it introduces babies to strong flavours from an early age. Adding some apple helps to tone down the strong flavour as well as adding a little sweetness. This purée freezes really well.

1 small swede
2 apples
2–4 tbsp breast milk or formula

Wash, peel, and chop the swede. Place in a steamer over boiling water and cook for 10–15 minutes, until partially tender.

Peel, core and chop or slice the apples. Add them to the steamer. Steam the swede and apple for about 10 minutes, until tender. Purée or mash with breast milk or formula.

You can either cover and refrigerate for up to 48 hours, or freeze in ice cube trays until solid, then transfer to a freezer bag, label, and use within 1 month. To defrost, simply remove 2 or 3 cubes of frozen swede and apple purée, allow to come to room temperature, stir and serve.

Makes 8–10 portions

papaya rice pudding

see variations page 51

Ripe papaya is easy to prepare and mash because of its high water content. Adding puréed brown rice to papaya makes a delicious fruity meal, a little like a baby version of a baked rice pudding. You could make rice pudding for the rest of the family and serve it with fresh papaya so the whole family would be eating the same pudding.

75 g (3 oz) uncooked brown rice　　　　　　**2–4 tbsp breast milk or formula**
225 ml (8 fl. oz) water
1 ripe papaya

Place the rice and water in a saucepan, bring to the boil, cover and simmer for 20 minutes, or until the liquid has been absorbed and the rice is cooked. Purée with a little breast milk or formula until the mixture is a thick, soupy consistency.

Halve the papaya, then scoop out and discard the black seeds. Scoop out the orange flesh and mash or purée.

Combine the cooked rice purée and papaya, adding a little more breast milk or formula as needed. Serve.

Make sure the rice is cooled for no more than 30 minutes at room temperature before placing in the refrigerator, and use within 24 hours. Cooled rice can be frozen immediately. Place in a freezerproof container, label and freeze for up to 1 month. To use from frozen, defrost thoroughly and heat through fully, then serve.

Makes 6–8 portions

variations

baby porridge

see base recipe page 27

banana baby porridge
Prepare the basic recipe, then add 1 teaspoon mashed banana. You may need to add more liquid.

apple baby porridge
Prepare the basic recipe, then stir in 1 teaspoon apple purée (page 30).

blueberry baby porridge
Prepare the basic recipe. Mash and strain 1 tablespoon fresh blueberries, then stir into the porridge.

fruity baby porridge
Prepare the basic recipe, then stir in a teaspoonful of a mixture of mashed banana and strained blueberries and a little more liquid if necessary.

baby porridge with apricots
Prepare the basic recipe. Meanwhile, cook 2–3 dried apricots in a little water until tender, purée and stir a teaspoonful into the porridge. Refrigerate or freeze the remaining apricot purée.

variations

melon purée

see base recipe page 29

melonocado
Mash ½ avocado with a slice of melon, adding a little breast milk or formula to achieve the required consistency.

melon & banana purée
Mash 1 banana with a slice of melon for a slightly thicker purée, and thin it down with a little breast milk or formula if required.

melon & apple purée
Prepare the basic recipe, adding 1 tablespoon apple purée (page 30).

melon & pear with cinnamon purée
Prepare the basic recipe, adding 1 tablespoon puréed fresh pear and a pinch of ground cinnamon.

melon & blueberry purée
Mash ½ cup fresh or thawed frozen blueberries, and press through a fine-mesh strainer to remove any seeds. Add to the melon, purée and serve as before.

apple purée

see base recipe page 30

apple & cinnamon purée
Prepare the basic recipe, adding 2 teaspoons ground cinnamon when cooking the apple.

purple purée
Prepare the basic recipe, but when the apple is almost cooked, add 75 g (3 oz) fresh or thawed frozen blueberries and continue cooking for 5 minutes before puréeing.

apple & pear purée
Prepare the basic recipe, adding 4 peeled, cored and chopped or sliced pears to the saucepan to cook with the apple.

mango & apple purée
Prepare the basic recipe. Purée 1 fresh mango. Stir into the apple purée.

apple & banana purée
Prepare the basic recipe, adding 1 mashed banana to the saucepan to cook with the apple.

variations

banana purée

see base recipe page 32

bananacado
Mash 2 ripe avocados with the banana, adding a little breast milk or formula to achieve the required consistency.

blue banana
Prepare the basic recipe. Lightly cook 4 tablespoons fresh blueberries in a little water for 5 minutes, until they collapse. Purée and press through a sieve, then stir into the mashed banana.

banapple
Instead of the basic recipe, add a little freshly squeezed apple juice to the banana instead of breast milk or formula.

peachy banana
Instead of the basic recipe, peel, pit and purée 2 ripe peaches. Add to the banana along with a little freshly squeezed apple juice to achieve the required consistency.

variations

mashed sweet potato

see base recipe page 34

sweet potato & leek
Prepare the basic recipe, using the steaming method. Add 2 chopped leeks (white part only) to the colander with the sweet potato. Purée with breast milk or formula.

green & orange swirly supper
Cook the sweet potatoes using the steaming method. Add 360 g (12½ oz) fresh baby spinach to the colander for the final 10 minutes of cooking time. Cook until tender. Purée the spinach and the sweet potato with breast milk or formula.

sweet potato & zucchini
Prepare the basic recipe, using the steaming method, and adding 2 courgettes, washed and chopped, to the colander with the sweet potatoes.

sweet potato & green beans
Prepare the basic recipe, using the steaming method, Add 55 g (2 oz) fresh or frozen green beans to the colander for the final 10 minutes of cooking.

sweet potato & carrot
Prepare the basic recipe, using the steaming method, and adding 2 peeled and chopped carrots to the colander with the sweet potatoes.

variations

mashed potato

see base recipe page 36

orange mash
Prepare the basic recipe. Wash, peel and chop 2 medium carrots, then steam or boil for 10–15 minutes, until tender. Mash or purée, and add to the mashed potato.

yellow mash
Prepare the basic recipe. Wash, peel and chop 1 swede, then steam or boil for 20–25 minutes, until tender. Mash or purée, and add to the mashed potato.

green mash
Cook the potatoes. Steam 225g (8 oz) fresh baby spinach leaves for 10 minutes, until tender, then purée with the potato and a little breast milk or formula.

pink mash
Prepare the basic recipe. Wash, peel, and chop 2 fresh beetroot. Steam or boil for 20–25 minutes until tender, then mash or purée and add to the mashed potato.

variations

mashed butternut squash

see base recipe page 39

butternut squash & sweet potato mash
Prepare the basic recipe, adding 1 washed, peeled and chopped sweet potato
to the steamer with the butternut squash.

butternut squash & carrot mash
Prepare the basic recipe, adding 1 washed, peeled and chopped medium carrot to
the steamer with the butternut squash.

popeye's squash
Prepare the basic recipe, adding 100 g (4 oz) fresh baby spinach to the steamer
for the last 10 minutes of cooking time. Add a pinch of ground nutmeg when
mashing or puréeing the vegetables.

squash & apple porridge
Prepare the basic recipe. Then stir in 1 tablespoon apple purée (page 30) and
1 tablespoon baby porridge (page 27).

butternut squash & cauliflower mash
Prepare the basic recipe, adding 5–6 washed cauliflower florets to the steamer
with the butternut squash.

variations

swede & apple purée

see base recipe page 40

swede, apple & carrot purée
Prepare the basic recipe, adding 1 washed, peeled and chopped medium carrot to the steamer with the swede.

swede & sweet potato mash
Prepare the basic recipe, replacing the apples with 1 washed, peeled, and chopped sweet potato. Add it to the steamer with the swede.

swede, apple & pumpkin mash
Prepare the basic recipe, adding the cubes from 1 peeled slice of pumpkin to the steamer with the swede.

swede, apple & parsnip mash
Prepare the basic recipe, adding 1 washed, peeled and chopped parsnip to the steamer with the swede.

variations

papaya rice pudding

see base recipe page 42

melon & papaya rice pudding
Prepare the basic recipe. Purée a slice of ripe cantaloupe or Galia melon and stir it into the pudding. Add a little breast milk or formula if necessary to achieve the required consistency.

peachy rice pudding
Prepare the basic recipe, but replace the papaya with 1 washed, peeled and pitted ripe peach.

apricot & papaya rice pudding
Prepare the basic recipe. Lightly cook 2–3 dried apricots in a little water for 5 minutes, until they soften. Purée, press through a sieve and stir into the papaya rice pudding.

apple & papaya rice pudding
Prepare the basic recipe. Peel, core and slice 1 apple. Cook it in a little water until tender, then purée and stir into the papaya rice pudding.

tropical fruit pudding
Prepare the basic recipe. Wash and pit 1 ripe mango. Mash or purée, then stir into the papaya rice pudding.

moving on: 6–9 months

Your baby can now eat virtually the same food as the rest of the family, with no added salt. Make sure you check that all ingredients are recommended for the age of your baby. Your baby will grow up knowing that everyone eats together.

banana yoghurt

see variations page 89

Once your baby is 6 months old, you can offer yoghurt for breakfast. Natural full-fat yoghurt is the best option. Sweeten and flavour it by adding puréed fresh fruit.

3 ripe bananas, peeled
6 tbsp natural full-fat yoghurt

Mash or purée the flesh of the banana with the yoghurt. As baby grows, leave the fruit with more lumps.

You can cover and refrigerate the banana yoghurt for 24 hours, but it tends to go brown quickly. Freeze banana yoghurt in ice cube trays until solid, then transfer to a freezer bag, label and use within 1 month. To defrost, simply remove 2 or 3 cubes of frozen banana yoghurt, allow to come to room temperature, stir and serve.

Makes 10–12 portions

scrambled eggs

see variations page 90

This is an easy introduction to eggs for babies over 6 months, which can be shared with the whole family. For babies close to 1 year, serve with toast fingers.

1 tsp butter
1–2 eggs, beaten

1 tbsp milk (use breast milk or formula for
babies under 12 months)

Melt the butter in a small saucepan or frying pan.

Beat the eggs with the milk. Once the butter has melted, tip in the eggs and stir constantly with a wooden spoon until thoroughly cooked.

Makes 1–2 portions

oat porridge

see variations page 91

Probably one of the easiest and most delicious breakfasts on the planet. After your
baby is 6 months old, you can introduce oats to his diet. As with any new foods, when
giving oats for the first time, monitor your baby's reaction to the food to check for
any allergies. It is possible to double up on quantities and refrigerate or freeze,
but it is just as quick to make fresh for each serving.

4 tbsp quick-cooking porridge oats
225 ml (8 fl. oz) milk (use breast milk or
    formula for babies under 12 months)

Put the oats and milk in a saucepan. Slowly bring to a boil, stirring continuously. Simmer for
5–6 minutes, until the oats are soft and the mixture is thick. Remove from heat. Add a little
extra cold breast milk or formula to cool and thin the porridge, if desired.

If you prefer, cook the porridge in a microwave. Heat on high for 1 minute, stir and heat
on high for another minute, stir and add cold breast milk or formula if desired.

Porridge should be eaten immediately, or cool at room temperature for no more than
1 hour, and freeze porridge in ice cube trays until solid. Transfer to a freezer bag, label
and use within 1 month. To defrost, simply remove 2 or 3 cubes of frozen porridge, allow
to come to room temperature, stir, heat through fully and serve.

Makes 4–8 portions

baby omelette

see variations page 92

An omelette cooked this way — flat, like a pancake — is fabulous as a finger food, so it's suitable for baby-led weaning, if desired.

1 tsp butter or a little olive oil
2 eggs, beaten

In a small frying pan set over medium heat, melt the butter or heat the olive oil. Pour in the eggs and shake so the eggs cover the bottom of the pan. Leave the pan on the burner and let the eggs set. Then, flip the omelette over, a little like a pancake, to thoroughly cook the other side.

Fold omelette over and cut into very small strips for baby, to serve.

Freeze extra portions in freezerproof containers, label and use within 1 month. To defrost, simply remove from the freezer, allow to come to room temperature, heat through fully and serve.

Makes 2–4 portions

french toast

see variations page 93

This is a true taste of childhood for many of us, which still tastes great to adults. But adults like their French toast (a.k.a. eggy bread) with butter, maple syrup and bacon. Babies under 1 year should not be given syrup or bacon, but they won't know what they're missing. They don't even need butter to enjoy their eggy bread, but it is good served with a couple of spoonfuls of apple purée (see recipe page 30).

6 eggs
6 tbsp milk (use breast milk or formula for
    under 12 months)

6 thick slices bread (crusts removed for
    younger ages)
a little butter

Beat the eggs with the milk. Pour mixture into a shallow, wide bowl or deep plate. Dunk each slice of bread into the egg mixture until it's totally coated. Repeat until all bread is coated in egg.

Heat the butter in a nonstick frying pan. Fry the bread until golden, turn over, and repeat with the other side. Remove from the pan and cut into fingers. One slice of bread will be sufficient for younger babies.

Place uncooked extra portions in a single layer on a greased baking tray and put in the freezer. When frozen, transfer to freezer bags, label and use within 1 month. To use from frozen, simply place the frozen french toast on a baking tray and bake at 220°C (425°F/ Gas mark 7) for 8 minutes, then turn and bake for an additional 10–12 minutes.

Makes 6 servings

spring vegetable soup

see variations page 94

As the name suggests, this soup is made with spring vegetables in season. It should be light and fresh-tasting. If you are making this for the whole family, double the quantities (for a family of 4–5).

2 medium carrots
2 leeks, white part only
½ head savoy cabbage

1 tsp. butter or a little olive oil
1 litre (35 fl. oz) cups low-sodium vegetable or chicken stock

Wash, peel and chop the carrots, leeks and cabbage. In a saucepan set over low heat, melt the butter or heat the olive oil. Add the vegetables and sauté for 5 minutes. Add the stock and bring to a boil. Cover the pan and simmer for 20–25 minutes, until the carrot is soft. Purée for babies up to 12 months.

Freeze extra portions in freezerproof containers, label and use within 3 months. To use from frozen, carefully defrost. Heat through fully before serving.

Makes 12–16 portions

leek & potato soup

see variations page 95

This is a lovely warming soup. The potatoes make it thick and easier for a baby to eat.
If you are making this for the whole family, double the quantities (for a family of 4–5).

1 potato
1 leek

1 tsp butter or a little olive oil
450 ml (16 fl. oz) low-sodium vegetable
  or chicken stock

Wash, peel and chop the potato and leek (white portion only).

In a large saucepan, melt the butter or heat the olive oil. Add the potatoes and leeks and
sauté for 5 minutes over low heat.

Add the stock and bring to a boil. Cover and simmer for 30 minutes, until the potato is soft.
Purée the mixture. Serve warm.

Freeze extra portions in freezerproof containers, label and use within 3 months. To use from
frozen, carefully defrost. Heat through fully before serving.

Makes 6–8 portions

chicken soup

see variations page 96

There are lots of stories about chicken soup being healing, and good for you if you have a cold. Chicken soup is definitely warming, and is very nutritious. Purée this soup for babies up to the age of 12 months; thereafter, make sure the chicken is chopped in very small pieces until your child is over 3 years old to prevent choking.

2 chicken portions (breast or leg)
2 carrots
2 small onions

2 stalks celery
900 ml (32 fl. oz) low-sodium chicken stock

Skin and chop the chicken. If the chicken is on the bone, then you can skin it and put it in whole. Finely chop the carrots, onions and celery. Add all the ingredients to the stock and bring to a boil. Cover and simmer for 30–40 minutes, until the vegetables are tender and the chicken is cooked.

Purée the soup and serve warm. If you used chicken on the bone, shred the meat from the bone and put it back in the soup before puréeing.

Freeze extra portions in small freezerproof containers, label and use within 1 month. To use from frozen, carefully defrost. Heat through fully before serving.

Makes 8–12 portions

classic tomato sauce

see variations page 97

A very versatile sauce full of antioxidants and vitamins from the tomatoes. Serve with cooked pasta, rice or use as a dip or pizza sauce (see page 211). Babies occasionally have an adverse reaction to tomatoes at this early stage, although others love them. Observe your baby carefully, and if there is any kind of allergic response, wait until after 12 months to reintroduce tomatoes.

2 tbsp olive oil
2 red or white onions, finely chopped
2 cloves garlic, finely chopped
16 ripe plum tomatoes, skinned and chopped,
   or 2 (400-g/14-oz.) tins whole plum
   tomatoes

450 ml (16 fl. oz) water
large handful of fresh basil leaves, washed
   and torn

Heat the oil in a frying pan or saucepan with a lid and gently sauté the onion over low to medium heat for 10–15 minutes, until it is translucent and soft.

Stir in the tomatoes and water. Bring to a boil, cover with the lid, reduce to a simmer and cook for 20 minutes. Remove the lid, stir in the basil leaves and simmer for a further 5 minutes, uncovered. Purée mixture in a blender or food processor.

Allow sauce to cool, then use or store in the refrigerator for up to 3 days, or freeze immediately and use within 1 month. To use from frozen, carefully defrost. Heat through fully before serving.

Makes 8–12 portions

mediterranean roasted vegetables

see variations page 98

This sauce is packed full of goodness, with its special selection of different-coloured vegetables to get the best mix of vitamins and minerals. This is a great sauce for all the family, and ideal to pour over cooked pasta.

1 red or white onion, roughly chopped
1 small aubergine, roughly chopped
1 small courgette, roughly chopped
1 red pepper, roughly chopped
1 orange pepper, roughly chopped

1 yellow or green pepper, chopped
1 tbsp olive oil
1 clove garlic, finely chopped
1 (400-g/14-oz) tin whole tomatoes
400 ml (14 fl. oz) low-sodium vegetable stock

Preheat the oven to 200°C (400°F/Gas mark 6). Place chopped vegetables on a baking pan, drizzle with the olive oil and sprinkle with the garlic. Roast for 20–25 minutes, turning them over halfway, until the vegetables are soft and slightly brown at the edges. Check the vegetables occasionally throughout the cooking time to make sure they don't burn. Transfer to a saucepan and add the tomatoes and vegetable stock. Bring to a boil, cover the pan and simmer for 20 minutes.

Purée in a food processor. If the sauce seems thin, reduce it slightly by boiling rapidly for 5 minutes, until it is thickened. For older babies (12 months +), and other members of the family, allow the sauce to have more lumps and serve with pasta or couscous, or in baked potatoes. Store in the refrigerator for up to 3 days, or freeze immediately and use within 1 month. To use from frozen, carefully defrost. Heat through fully before serving.

Makes 6–8 child portions or 3–4 adult portions

carrot & chicken dinner

see variations page 99

Chicken is mild in flavour and a good form of protein to start your baby on. When it is puréed, however, it can be quite thick, so it will need a lot of liquid to thin it to a consistency easy for your baby to swallow. Adding root vegetables such as carrots helps make the chicken more palatable. If your baby is low in iron, replace the chicken breast with thigh meat, which is higher in iron.

2 skinless and boneless chicken breasts
2 carrots, washed, peeled and chopped

breast milk or formula, as needed

Poaching is an ideal way of cooking chicken because the chicken stays moist, is easy to purée and retains most of its nutrients. Preheat the oven to 190°C (375°F/Gas mark 5). Place the chicken in a baking dish with 1 cm (½ in) of boiling water. Add the chopped carrot, making sure it is covered with water, and cover the dish with kitchen foil. Cook for 20–30 minutes, or until the chicken is cooked through. Do not let it overcook or it will be tough. Remove the chicken and carrot from the liquid, and purée with breast milk or formula, or some of the cooking liquid, to the desired consistency. If you want to steam the chicken, place it and the chopped carrot in a steamer over boiling water. Steam for 20–30 minutes, until the chicken is cooked through. Purée with a little breast milk or formula.

Store in the refrigerator for up to 2 days, or freeze immediately and use within 1 month. To use from frozen, carefully defrost. Heat through fully before serving.

Makes 8–10 child portions

turkey casserole

see variations page 100

This classic casserole includes lots of vegetables. It is a great meal for the whole family and easily adjusted for young babies.

1 tbsp sunflower oil	450 g (1 lb) thinly sliced turkey breast cutlets
1 onion	1 tsp chopped fresh thyme
2 carrots	225 ml (8 fl. oz) low-sodium chicken stock

Preheat the oven to 175°C (350°F/Gas mark 4). Heat the oil in a nonstick frying pan. Peel and finely chop the onion and carrots. Brown the turkey in the oil, turning often until all sides are coloured. Transfer to a heavy casserole dish and add the remaining ingredients. Bring to the boil, cover with a lid, transfer to the oven and cook for 40–45 minutes, until the turkey is cooked through.

Remove from the oven, purée for babies under 9 months, or cut up the turkey pieces for babies under 12 months. Serve with mashed potato or rice (puréed for babies).

Store in the refrigerator for up to 2 days, or freeze immediately and use within 1 month. To use from frozen, carefully defrost. Heat through fully before serving.

Makes 6–8 child portions or 2 adult portions

beef goulash

see variations page 101

This Hungarian dish combines inexpensive cuts of beef with potatoes for a hearty warming stew. Goulash is even better eaten the day after it is made, because the potatoes break down, thickening the stew, and the flavours are absorbed, leaving a thick, comforting dish. If you want, you can make this goulash in a slow cooker.

1 onion
1 tbsp sunflower oil
3 fresh tomatoes or 1 (225-g/8-oz) tin chopped
    tomatoes
½ small red pepper

1 tsp mild paprika
285 g (10½ oz) lean steak for braising, finely
    sliced
225 ml (8 fl. oz) low-sodium beef stock
225 g (8 oz) potatoes, peeled and chopped

Peel and finely chop the onion. Heat the oil in a nonstick frying pan and fry the onion over low to medium heat for 10 minutes, until soft and translucent. Transfer to a baking dish with a lid that can be used on the hob. Peel, deseed and chop the fresh tomatoes and add to the dish. (If using tinned tomatoes, just pour in the tomatoes and their juices.) Finely chop the pepper and add to the baking dish along with the paprika. Cook for 3–4 minutes over low to medium heat. Add the steak slices to the dish, cook for 2–3 minutes, then add the stock. Bring to the boil, and reduce to a simmer. Add the potatoes to the pan. Put on the lid, and cook for 2 hours on the hob or in the oven at 160°C (325°F/Gas mark 3). Allow to cool a little, then purée before serving.

Store in the refrigerator for up to 2 days, or freeze immediately and use within 1 month. To use from frozen, carefully defrost. Heat through fully before serving.

Makes 8–10 child portions or 2 adult portions

chicken curry & rice

see variations page 102

This is a basic chicken curry recipe using classic Indian spices. Purée the rice for babies under 9 months (see page 25) to avoid choking hazard.

1 tbsp sunflower oil
1 (1-cm/^{1}/$_2$-inch) piece root ginger, peeled and
    finely chopped
1 clove garlic, peeled and finely chopped
^{1}/$_2$ small onion, peeled and finely chopped
^{1}/$_2$ tsp ground cumin
^{1}/$_2$ tsp ground coriander
pinch ground cinnamon

1 boneless, skinless chicken breast, chopped
1 carrot, peeled and chopped
1 (225-g/8-oz) tin chopped tomatoes
100 ml (4 fl. oz) low-sodium chicken or
    vegetable stock
1 tbsp plain full-fat yoghurt
1 tbsp washed and finely chopped
    fresh coriander

Heat the oil in a nonstick frying pan. Blend the ginger, garlic and onion in a food processor. Add a tablespoon of water if the paste is very thick. Transfer to the frying pan and cook on medium–low heat for 5 minutes. Stir in the cumin, coriander and cinnamon. Cook for 2–3 minutes.

Stir-fry the chicken in the curry sauce for 3–4 minutes until coloured. Add the carrot to the curry along with the tomatoes and stock, reduce to a simmer, and cover. Cook for 15–20 minutes, until the carrots are soft and the chicken cooked through. Purée for babies under 9 months. Just before serving, swirl in the yoghurt and sprinkle the coriander on top.

Discard any uneaten rice. Store the curry in the refrigerator for up to 2 days, or freeze immediately and use within 1 month. To use from frozen, carefully defrost. Heat through

Makes 8 child portions or 2 adult portions

beef stew

see variations page 103

Choose lean cuts of beef or lean minced beef for this stew. Red meat is a good source
of easily absorbed iron, which babies need for growth and brain development. This
stew freezes well.

450 g (1 lb) lean cubed or lean minced beef
1 tsp dried mixed herbs

2 carrots, washed, peeled and chopped
2 potatoes, washed, peeled and chopped

Put the beef into a saucepan with the herbs, then add enough water to cover. Add
the chopped carrots and potatoes to the pan. Cover, bring to the boil and simmer for
20–25 minutes, or until the meat and vegetables are cooked.

Drain the water and reserve. Purée the beef and vegetables, adding the cooking water as
needed to achieve the required consistency. Serve warm.

Store in the refrigerator for up to 2 days. Cool the mixture quickly and refrigerate within
1 hour, or freeze immediately and use within 1 month. To use from frozen, carefully defrost.
Heat through fully before serving.

Makes 8–10 child portions

moussaka

see variations page 104

A traditional Greek dish of minced lamb and aubergine, topped with a béchamel sauce.

2 tbsp sunflower oil, divided
1 onion, peeled and finely chopped
1 carrot, peeled and finely chopped
1 garlic clove, peeled and finely chopped
275 g (10 oz) lean minced lamb
1 tsp each fresh oregano & thyme
½ tsp each ground cinnamon & allspice

1 (400-g/14-oz) tin chopped tomatoes
225 ml (8 fl. oz) low-sodium lamb or beef stock
1 tsp tomato paste
1 aubergine, cut into 1-cm (½-in) slices
1 quantity cheese sauce (page 191)
1 egg, beaten

Heat 1 tablespoon oil in a nonstick frying pan over medium heat. Sauté the onion, carrot and garlic until softened. Transfer to a large saucepan with lid. Break up the lamb and add to the pan with the herbs and spices. Cook for 4–5 minutes, until slightly browned, stirring constantly. Transfer to the saucepan. Over medium heat, mix in the tomatoes and juices, stock and tomato paste. Bring to the boil. Reduce to a simmer, cover and cook for 1 hour. Meanwhile, heat the remaining oil in the frying pan, and fry the aubergine over medium heat until golden brown. Drain on kitchen towels. Make the cheese sauce (page 191), add the beaten egg and mix well. Preheat the oven to 200°C (400°F/Gas mark 6). Place a layer of aubergine in a baking dish, cover with the meat sauce, add the remaining aubergine, and top with cheese sauce. Bake for 45–60 minutes until golden brown. Purée for young babies.

Store in the refrigerator for up to 2 days, or freeze immediately and use within 1 month. To use from frozen, carefully defrost. Heat through fully before serving.

Makes 8 child portions or 2–3 adult portions

apple & mango sorbet

see variations page 105

A sorbet is a water ice rather than an ice cream. This version is made without sugar. It is deliciously refreshing on a hot day and a good way to encourage children to taste different flavours and consume fruit.

1 large mango, peeled and stoned
50 ml (2 fl. oz) fresh unsweetened apple juice

Put the mango and apple juice in a blender and purée.

To freeze with an ice cream maker: follow the manufacturer's instructions, then transfer to a freezer container and set in the freezer for 30 minutes to firm up before serving.

To freeze without an ice cream maker: pour the mixture into a suitable freezer container and place in the freezer. After 1 hour, remove the container, pour the contents into a bowl and whisk to break down the ice crystals. This step is necessary so that you end up with a smooth texture. Pour the mixture back into the freezer container and freeze. Repeat every hour for the next 4 hours, then the sorbet will be ready to serve.

Store in the freezer for no longer than 1 week. Place the container in the refrigerator 30 minutes before you wish to eat it as it will be very hard.

Makes 1 ½ pints

baked apples

see variations page 106

This was the first food my daughter tried when I was weaning her. I sat next to her chair eating a baked apple while trying to feed her baby rice. She kept leaning forward trying to reach my spoon. I let her try a little of my apple and she loved it. She's a teenager now and still loves baked apples.

6 apples
1 tsp. light brown sugar (optional)

Preheat the oven to 200°C (400°F/Gas mark 6). Wash and core the apples, stuff the sugar into the hollowed-out core (adding the sugar is optional), then score the skin horizontally around the middle. Place in an ovenproof dish and bake for 30–35 minutes, until the apple is soft and the flesh has slightly exploded through the scored skin.

Scoop out the flesh and serve warm or cold. Serve it on its own to a baby, or with a little homemade custard, cream or ice cream to older children and adults.

Once cool, baked apples can be stored in the refrigerator for 2 days. The mashed flesh can be frozen for up to 1 month. Freeze in ice cube trays until solid, then transfer to a suitable freezerproof container and label. To defrost, simply remove 2 or 3 cubes of frozen apple mash, allow to come to room temperature, stir and serve.

Makes 6–10 child portions

baked bananas

see variations page 107

Bananas can be baked in the oven or grilled outdoors. They are delicious with vanilla ice cream and are just as nice on their own. They are lovely hot or cold.

6 bananas
pinch ground cinnamon
6 tsp butter

Preheat the oven to 220°C (425°F/Gas mark 7). Slit the banana peel lengthwise on the inside of the curve. Gently ease the banana out, leaving the skin intact. Sprinkle with the cinnamon and dot with the butter.

Put the banana back in the skin and wrap in kitchen foil. Put it directly on the oven rack and bake for 25–30 minutes, until the banana is soft and the skin is blackened. (If the banana is very ripe, reduce the cooking time to 20–25 minutes.)

Scoop out the flesh, mash and serve. Once cold, store in the refrigerator for 24 hours. The mashed banana can be frozen for up to 1 month. Freeze in ice cube trays until solid, then transfer to a suitable freezerproof container and label. To defrost, simply remove 2 or 3 cubes of frozen banana mash and allow to come to room temperature, stir and serve.

Makes 6–12 child portions

banana yoghurt

see base recipe page 53

bananacado yoghurt
Prepare the basic recipe, adding ½ ripe avocado and mashing it in. Add a little breast milk or formula to achieve the required consistency.

banapple yoghurt
Prepare the basic recipe, adding 1 tablespoon apple purée (page 30).

blueberry yoghurt pudding
Lightly cook 1 tablespoon fresh or thawed frozen blueberries in a little water for 5 minutes until they collapse. Purée and press through a sieve, then stir into the mashed banana before mixing with the yoghurt.

melonana pudding
Prepare the basic recipe, adding 1 puréed slice of peeled ripe cantaloupe or Galia melon.

peachy pudding
Prepare the basic recipe, adding 1 washed, peeled, pitted and puréed ripe peach.

variations

scrambled eggs

see base recipe page 54

scrambled eggs with cheese
Prepare the basic recipe, adding 25 g (1 oz) finely grated Cheddar cheese to the eggs as you beat them with the milk.

scrambled eggs with spinach
Prepare the basic recipe, adding 6–7 chopped fresh baby spinach leaves to the eggs at the start of cooking. The spinach will wilt and cook along with the eggs.

scrambled eggs with puréed vegetables
Prepare the basic recipe, adding a cube (1 tablespoon) of puréed vegetables such as carrots, broccoli or sweet potato to the scrambled eggs once cooked.

scrambled eggs with salmon
Prepare the basic recipe, adding a tablespoonful of cooked, mashed salmon to the scrambled eggs once cooked.

scrambled eggs with tomato
Prepare the basic recipe, adding 1 fresh tomato. Put the tomato in a bowl, cover with boiling water and leave for 10 minutes. The skin will split, making it easy for you to remove it. Remove the skin and seeds, and mash before stirring into the scrambled eggs.

oat porridge

see base recipe page 56

porridge with apple
Prepare the basic recipe. Just before serving, wash, peel, core and grate 1 apple, and stir it into the cooked porridge.

peachy porridge
Prepare the basic recipe. Stir 1 washed, peeled, pitted and puréed ripe peach through the cooked porridge with a pinch of ground cinnamon.

porridge with apricot purée
Prepare the basic recipe. Cook 2–3 apricots in a little water for 4–5 minutes until plump, then purée and add to the porridge.

porridge with raisins
Prepare the basic recipe. Cook 2 teaspoons raisins in a little water until plump, then purée and add to the cooked porridge.

porridge with pear
Prepare the basic recipe. Just before serving, wash, peel, core and grate 1 ripe pear, and stir it into the cooked porridge.

variations

baby omelette

see base recipe page 58

herby baby omelette
Prepare the basic recipe. Chop 1 teaspoon fresh herbs and sprinkle them over the omelette before you flip it over.

cheesy baby omelette
Prepare the basic recipe. Sprinkle 1 tablespoon grated hard cheese such as Cheddar over the omelette after you've flipped it over.

baby spinach omelette
Prepare the basic recipe, sprinkling 6–7 chopped fresh baby spinach leaves onto the omelette before it sets.

ham & cheese omelette
Prepare the basic recipe. Sprinkle 1 tablespoon grated cheese, such as Cheddar, and slices of lean wafer-thin ham onto the omelette before it sets. Check that it has thoroughly cooked before folding it over.

baby omelette with pea purée
Prepare the basic recipe, but give it a lovely green sandwich effect. Cook 50 g (2 oz) frozen peas in a little water for 5 minutes until tender, then purée. Spread the pea purée over the cooked omelette before folding it, then cut it into strips.

variations

french toast

see base recipe page 61

french toast with fresh fruit purée
Prepare the basic recipe. Serve with a bit of apple and pear, or apple and mango purée (see page 45).

french toast with grated cheese
Prepare the basic recipe, adding 1 heaping tablespoon finely grated hard cheese, such as Cheddar, to the egg and milk mixture.

french toast with ham
Prepare the basic recipe. Top the cooked fingers with fingers of lean ham, and serve.

french toast with herbs
Prepare the basic recipe, adding 1 teaspoon chopped fresh herbs to the egg mixture before cooking.

french toast with worcestershire sauce (12 months +)
Prepare the basic recipe, adding ½ teaspoon Worcestershire sauce to the egg mixture before cooking. (Worcestershire sauce introduces a new, gently spicy flavour to the baby, but use only a very small amount because it is high in salt.)

variations

spring vegetable soup

see base recipe page 62

spring vegetable soup with potatoes
Prepare the basic recipe, adding 1 peeled and chopped potato to the other vegetables for a thicker, more filling soup. Purée as before.

spring vegetable soup with peas
Prepare the basic recipe, adding 1 tablespoon fresh or frozen peas in the last 5 minutes of cooking. Peas will sweeten the soup, but it will still have its 'spring-like' freshness. Purée as before.

spring vegetable soup with courgette
Prepare the basic recipe, adding 1 small courgette, washed and grated, to the other vegetables. Purée as before.

spring vegetable soup with red pepper
Prepare the basic recipe, adding 1 small red pepper, chopped, to the other vegetables. Purée as before.

variations

leek & potato soup

see base recipe page 64

cock-a-leekie
Prepare the basic recipe, adding the chopped meat from 1 chicken thigh to the pan with the potato and leek.

leek & potato soup with carrots
Prepare the basic recipe, adding 1 peeled and chopped small carrot to the pan with the potato and leek.

leek & potato soup with cabbage
Prepare the basic recipe, adding ¼ head of Savoy cabbage to the pan with the potato and leek.

vichyssoise
Prepare the basic soup. Purée and chill it. Serve cold with a little crème fraîche stirred in or swirled on top.

leek & sweet potato soup
Prepare the basic recipe, replacing the potato with one large or two small sweet potatoes.

variations

chicken soup

see base recipe page 67

chicken & corn soup
Prepare the basic recipe, adding 100 g (4 oz) corn kernels (fresh, frozen or tinned) in the last 5 minutes of cooking.

chicken & mushroom soup
Prepare the basic recipe, adding 6 finely chopped button mushrooms with the other vegetables.

chicken noodle soup (12 months +)
Prepare the basic recipe, adding 25 g (1 oz) spaghetti broken up into small pieces in the last 10 minutes of cooking time. Make sure the vegetables and chicken flesh are chopped very small, as you don't purée this soup variation so it's not suitable for babies under 12 months.

thai chicken soup (12 months +)
Prepare the basic recipe, adding 2 stalks of fresh lemongrass cut lengthways and 2 kaffir lime leaves, and adding 2 tablespoons fresh or frozen peas and 1 tablespoon fish sauce in the last 5 minutes of cooking.

classic tomato sauce

see base recipe page 69

gazpacho (12 months +)
Prepare the basic recipe and chill completely. Stir in ½ finely chopped or grated cucumber, ½ finely chopped red or orange pepper and a pinch of ground cumin and chilli powder (optional). Thin the sauce down to a soup consistency by adding 225 ml (8 fl. oz) cold water. Serve with ice cubes floating in each bowl.

tomato dipping sauce
Prepare the basic recipe. After adding the basil, cook the sauce for a further 20 minutes until it has thickened, stirring frequently so it does not burn. Serve warm or cold, with vegetable sticks and breadsticks (page 130) for older babies.

tomato soup
Prepare the basic recipe, replace the water with 450 ml (16 fl. oz) vegetable stock, purée and serve warm.

ketchup (12 months +)
Prepare the basic recipe, omitting the basil and adding a pinch of ground ginger. Cook the sauce without the lid and raise the heat for the last 5 minutes of cooking time to reduce the sauce to a thick, ketchup consistency.

variations

mediterranean roasted vegetables

see base recipe page 70

stuffed aubergines with roasted vegetable sauce
Prepare the basic recipe. Meanwhile, halve 2 aubergines, brush with olive oil, and roast for 30 minutes at 220°C (425°F/Gas mark 7), cut-side down, until soft. Scoop out the flesh, leaving the skin whole. Chop or mash the flesh, mix with half the sauce, and fill the aubergine skins. Sprinkle with a little mozzarella cheese and grill for 3–4 minutes.

roasted vegetable sauce pasta bake
Prepare the basic recipe and mix with 350 g (12 oz) cooked pasta. Preheat the oven to 190°C (375°F/Gas mark 5), transfer the pasta and sauce to an ovenproof baking dish, sprinkle with grated cheese and bake for 10 minutes.

roasted vegetable sauce with meatballs
Prepare the basic recipe. Stir in meatballs made from minced beef or lamb (page 208), cook through until piping hot and serve over pasta.

roasted vegetable sauce on garlic bread (9 months +)
Prepare the basic recipe. Thickly slice some bread, brush with olive oil, and rub with a peeled garlic clove. Toast the bread under the grill, spread with spoonfuls of the sauce, sprinkle with mozzarella cheese and serve.

chicken & carrot dinner

see base recipe page 72

chicken, carrot & potato dinner
Prepare the basic recipe, adding 1 peeled and chopped potato.

chicken, carrot & parsnip dinner
Prepare the basic recipe, adding 1 peeled and chopped parsnip.

chicken, sweet potato & spinach dinner
Prepare the basic recipe, adding 100 g (4 oz) fresh spinach leaves to the chicken and replacing the carrot with 1 steamed or baked mashed sweet potato (page 34).

chicken, lentil & sweet potato dinner (9 months +)
Instead of the basic recipe, put the chopped chicken breast in a pan with 1 washed, peeled and chopped sweet potato and 50 g (2 oz) red lentils. Cover with water, bring to the boil and cook for 30–35 minutes. Purée or mash with a little breast milk or formula.

herby chicken dinner
Instead of the basic recipe, put the chopped chicken breast and carrot in a saucepan with 1 peeled and chopped parsnip and potato and a pinch of dried herbs of your choice. Cover with water, bring to the boil, and simmer for 20–25 minutes. Purée or mash with a little breast milk or formula.

variations

turkey casserole

see base recipe page 75

turkey casserole with mushrooms
Prepare the basic recipe, adding 6 finely chopped mushrooms at the same time as the carrots.

turkey casserole with leeks
Prepare the basic recipe, replacing the onion with 1 washed and finely chopped leek, white part only, at the same time as the carrots.

turkey casserole with potato
Prepare the basic recipe, adding 1 peeled and chopped medium potato at the same as the carrots.

turkey casserole with swede & sweet potato
Prepare the basic recipe, replacing the carrots with 1 small swede and 1 small sweet potato, washed, peeled and chopped.

turkey casserole with pepper
Prepare the basic recipe, replacing the carrots with 2 chopped red or green peppers.

variations

beef goulash

300 base recipe page 76

beef goulash with rice
Prepare the basic recipe, using 100 g (4 oz) of potatoes , purée and serve the goulash with puréed rice. Leave the dish and rice unpuréed for babies over 9 months.

pork goulash
Prepare the basic recipe, replacing the beef with boneless pork.

beef goulash with mushrooms & carrots
Prepare the basic recipe, replacing the green pepper with a few finely chopped mushrooms and 1 washed, peeled and finely chopped carrot. Purée or mash, and serve as before.

chicken goulash
Prepare the basic recipe, replacing the beef with 2–3 boneless, skinless chicken breasts. Purée or mash and serve as before.

vegetable goulash
Prepare the basic recipe, replacing the beef with ½ an aubergine, finely chopped, and replace the beef stock with low-sodium vegetable stock. Heat the aubergine in the frying pan along with the onion, and prepare as before.

variations

chicken curry with rice

see base recipe page 79

chicken curry with raisins (9 months +)
Prepare the basic recipe, adding 1 tablespoon raisins to the curry at the same time as the stock. Make sure the raisins are mashed or very finely chopped to avoid choking hazard.

cauliflower & potato curry
Prepare the basic recipe, replacing the chicken and carrot with a few washed cauliflower florets and 1 washed, peeled and chopped small potato. Purée or mash as before.

sweet potato & peas curry
Prepare the basic recipe, replacing the chicken with 1 washed, peeled and chopped small sweet potato and 1 tablespoon frozen peas. Purée or mash as before.

chicken & mango curry
Prepare the basic recipe, adding ½ peeled and chopped ripe mango to the recipe 5 minutes before the end of the cooking time. Purée or mash as before.

beef stew

see base recipe page 80

lamb stew

Prepare the basic recipe, replacing the beef with 225 g (½ lb) of boneless lamb cubes or minced lamb.

pork stew

Prepare the basic recipe, replacing the beef with 225 g (½ lb) pound of boneless pork cubes or minced pork.

chicken stew

Prepare the basic recipe, replacing the beef with 2–3 boneless, skinless chicken breasts.

beef stew with broccoli & green beans

Prepare the basic recipe. Add 4 broccoli florets and a handful of green beans to the pot with the meat, potato, and carrot during the last 10 minutes of cooking.

beef stew with brown rice

Prepare the basic recipe, omitting the potato. Cook 140 g (5 oz) brown rice in 240 ml (8½ fl. oz) water for 15–20 minutes, until the water has been absorbed and the rice is tender. Add rice to the beef and carrot, and purée.

variations

moussaka

see base recipe page 83

moussaka with potato slices
Prepare the basic recipe, replacing the aubergine with 3 medium potatoes, washed, peeled and cut into thick slices. Purée or mash for younger babies, or serve as is for babies over 12 months.

beef moussaka
Prepare the basic recipe, replacing the minced lamb with lean minced beef. Purée or mash, and serve.

vegetable moussaka (9 months +)
Prepare the basic recipe, replacing the meat with 100 g (4 oz) green lentils and adding 1 deseeded and finely chopped red pepper to the onion. Purée or mash, and serve.

turkey moussaka
Prepare the basic recipe, replacing the lamb with minced turkey. Purée or mash, and serve.

apple and mango sorbet

see base recipe page 84

apple and peach sorbet
Prepare the basic recipe, omitting the mango and using 3 large ripe peaches, peeled, pitted and chopped. Purée the peaches with the apple juice, and freeze.

apple and pear sorbet
Prepare the basic recipe, omitting the mango and using 2 large ripe pears, peeled, cored and chopped. Purée the pears with the apple juice, and freeze.

apple and grape sorbet
Prepare the basic recipe, omitting the mango and using 200 g (7 oz) seedless grapes, peeled and mashed. Purée the grapes with the apple juice, and freeze.

lime and mango sorbet (12 months +)
Prepare the basic recipe, replacing the apple juice with 50 ml (2 fl. oz) freshly squeezed lime juice. If this needs to be sweetened, add a teaspoon of honey.

lemon and mango sorbet (12 months +)
Prepare the basic recipe, replacing the apple juice with 50 ml (2 fl. oz) freshly squeezed lemon juice. If this needs to be sweetened, add a teaspoon of honey.

baked apples

see base recipe page 87

cinnamon-baked apples with frozen yoghurt
Prepare the basic recipe, mixing in 1 teaspoon cinnamon with the brown sugar. Serve warm with a scoop of sugar-free frozen yoghurt.

baked apples with orange & apricot
Prepare the basic recipe, adding 1 chopped dried apricot to the hollowed-out core. Sprinkle with the grated zest of 1 orange and drizzle with the juice from the orange before baking.

baked apples with pear
Prepare the basic recipe. Mix the brown sugar with the mashed flesh of 1 pear, and stuff it into the hollowed-out core.

baked pears with blueberries
Instead of the basic recipe, core 6 pears, and place in a baking tray. Fill the hollowed-out cores with blueberries. Bake at 200°C (400°F/Gas mark 6) for 15–20 minutes. Cool before serving, and purée for young babies.

baked peaches
Prepare the basic recipe, substituting the apple with one large, ripe, stoned peach.

variations

baked bananas

see base recipe page 88

baked bananas with brown sugar and chopped nuts (12 months +)
Prepare the basic recipe, sprinkle a teaspoon of brown sugar on the banana,
dot with butter and cook as instructed. Sprinkle with finely chopped/ground
nuts to serve.

baked bananas with frozen yoghurt
Prepare the basic recipe, serve warm with a scoop of sugar-free frozen yoghurt.

baked bananas with chocolate chips (12 months +)
Prepare the basic recipe, replacing the cinnamon and butter with a teaspoon
of chocolate chips placed inside the skin next to the banana. Serve warm as
the chocolate will have melted.

baked bananas with sweetened ricotta cheese
Prepare the basic recipe, mix a teaspoon of icing sugar with a tablespoon
of ricotta cheese, and serve with the warm banana.

pre-toddler: 9–12 months

Babies are starting to assert their independence, trying to feed themselves. Milk teeth may be coming through, making it easier for babies to bite. It's time to introduce textures, so don't purée their food quite as much. Be careful of choking hazards such as whole grapes or berries and cubes of hard fruit and vegetables. Enjoy being more adventurous!

potato farls

see variations page 142

This is a good way to use up leftover mashed potatoes. Potato farls are from Ireland and are sometimes known as potato cakes or tattie bread. They are a lovely alternative to sandwiches for toddlers. Cut them into small pieces to serve as a snack for babies and toddlers.

900 g (2 lb) mashed potatoes
150 g (5 oz) plain flour

2 tbsp butter, melted

In a large bowl, mix together all the ingredients. Transfer to a lightly floured work surface and knead lightly until everything is well mixed and the mixture is smooth.

With a rolling pin, roll out the mixture into a rough circle about the size of a dinner plate, and cut into quarters (these are the farls), or smaller slices for babies under 12 months.

Heat a heavy-based frying pan over medium–high heat, add a little butter, and swirl it around to coat the bottom of the pan. Place the farls into the hot butter and cook for 3–4 minutes until golden brown. Turn and cook the other side. Remove from the heat and cover with a clean tea towel. If covered, they can be kept warm in a low oven for up to 30–40 minutes.

Potato farls are best eaten when warm. If you do want to make them in advance, freeze them as soon as they are cool, defrost thoroughly and heat through fully before serving. If frozen, use within 1 month.

Makes 8 potato farls

biscotti with babyccino

see variations page 143

Biscotti are very hard, twice-baked Italian biscuits, which are ideal for dunking in frothy warm milk (a babyccino). For adults, serve with cappuccino or hot chocolate.

250 g (9 oz) plain flour
2 tsp baking powder
½ tsp ground cinnamon
2 eggs, whisked

1 egg yolk
1 tbsp milk (use breast milk or formula for
   babies under 12 months)

Preheat the oven to 175°C (350°F/Gas mark 4). Grease and line a baking tray. Mix together the flour, baking powder and cinnamon in a large bowl. If making for adults, add 175 g (6 oz) sugar to this mixture. Stirring the dry ingredients, add enough egg so that the mixture comes together to form a soft dough. Do not add all the beaten egg as you may not need all of it. If you add too much, add a little more flour. Split the dough into two pieces, and shape each piece into a log shape. Place the logs on the baking tray and flatten the top of each. Beat together the egg yolk and milk. With a pastry brush, paint each log with the mixture to glaze. When cooked, the glaze will give the biscotti a shiny finish. Bake the logs for 20–25 minutes until golden brown. Remove from the oven and allow to cool. Turn the oven down to 160°C (325°F/Gas mark 3). Using a very sharp serrated knife, slice the logs across at 1-cm (½-in) intervals. Lay biscotti on the baking tray, cut-side down, in a single layer. Bake for 15–20 minutes, until dried and golden brown. Remove from the oven and cool on a wire rack.

Keep in an airtight container for up to 1 week, or freeze the day they are made for up to 1 month. If freezing, defrost thoroughly and heat through fully before serving.
Makes 20–24 biscotti

baby crêpes

see variations page 144

Batter crêpes are delicious with fresh fruit and are very easy to make. Crêpes
are ideal finger foods for a baby 9 months and older. Drizzle the crêpes
with a little freshly squeezed orange juice.

75 g (3 oz) plain flour
1 egg, beaten

225 ml (8 fl. oz) milk (use breast milk or
formula for babies under 12 months)
1 tsp butter

Put the flour in a bowl, make a well in the centre and pour in the beaten egg. Using a whisk
to beat the egg into the flour, start in the middle and gradually add flour from around the
edges. Add the milk little by little, making sure you have a smooth batter before adding
more. Repeat until all the milk is incorporated.

Melt the butter in a non-stick frying pan over medium heat. Pour in enough batter to cover
the bottom of the pan. Once the edges begin to lift, turn the crêpe over and cook the other
side. Once it starts to bubble, it is ready. Remove to a warm plate, cover with a clean tea
towel or kitchen foil, and repeat until all the batter is used up. Cut into strips for baby. The
rest of the family can have big crêpes made from batter using cow's milk rather than breast
milk or formula.

Keep in an airtight container wrapped in clingfilm for up to 2 days in the refrigerator, or
freeze the day they are made for up to 1 month. If freezing, defrost thoroughly and heat
through fully before serving.

Makes 4 crêpes

cheesy mash

see variations page 145

A very adaptable dish to serve with meat, chicken, fish or just on its own with some fresh vegetables. You could roll the potato mash into 2.5-cm (1-in) balls to give to your baby or toddler. If you find the mash is sticky to roll, then dip your fingers in a little flour. Babies love cheesy mash balls.

2 medium potatoes
4 tbsps grated cheese

Preheat the oven to 220°C (425°F/Gas mark 7).

Prick the potatoes all over using a fork, put on the top rack of the oven and bake for 50–60 minutes until soft in the middle.

Remove from the oven, slit down the middle and scoop out the potato into a bowl. Add the grated cheese and mash. Either spoon back into the skin of the potato or serve as it is.

Store in the refrigerator for 3 days, or in the freezer for up to 1 month. Freeze them as soon as they are cool, defrost thoroughly and heat through fully before serving.

Makes 6–8 portions

oven-baked potato wedges

see variations page 146

Healthier than chips, these are baked in the oven and can be eaten with dips or as a side vegetable. They are a great finger food for 9-month-old babies.

6 large potatoes
6 tsp sunflower oil

Preheat the oven to 220°C (425°F/Gas mark 7).

Wash and peel the potatoes, cut in half lengthwise, and then into 8–10 wedges, depending on the size of the potatoes.

Pour the sunflower oil into a freezer-weight bag. Add the potatoes, secure the top, and shake so that the oil coats the potato wedges. (This means that you are adding far less oil than if you drizzled the oil over the wedges on a baking tray.)

Lay the potato wedges on a baking tray and bake for 20–25 minutes, turning halfway through so they cook evenly. They are cooked when golden brown on the outside and soft in the middle. Remove from the oven and allow to cool a little before serving.

They will keep in the refrigerator for up to 2 days or for up to 1 month in the freezer. If freezing, defrost thoroughly and heat through fully before serving.

Makes 6–8 portions

dhal

see variations page 147

Lentils are high in protein, low in fat and contain calcium, iron and fibre. The baby
should have been eating fruit and vegetables for 1–2 months before moving on to
lentils. Red lentils are the easiest to digest. Lentils may give your baby gas, so try a small
amount of dhal first time. If there are no adverse effects, next time give a little more.

50 g (2 oz) red lentils
1 small onion
a little sunflower oil
2-cm (¾-in) piece root ginger, peeled
    and grated

1 clove garlic, finely chopped
½ tsp ground coriander
¼ tsp ground cinnamon
¼ tsp ground turmeric
400 ml (14 fl. oz) low-sodium vegetable stock

Soak the lentils for 1 hour, drain, rinse and simmer them in fresh water for 10 minutes,
then drain and rinse again, before proceeding with the recipe. Place the lentils in a bowl
and cover with water to soak while you prepare the onion. Peel and finely chop or grate
the onion. Heat a little sunflower oil in a saucepan, then sauté the onion over a gentle heat
for 10–15 minutes until it becomes translucent. Add the root ginger and garlic and cook for
1 minute. Add the coriander, cinnamon and turmeric, and cook for another minute. Drain the
lentils, rinse and add to the pan. Pour in the stock, bring to the boil, cover and simmer for
20–30 minutes until the lentils are tender. Check on the dhal regularly. If it looks dry, add
more stock or water.

Allow to cool slightly and serve, or store in the refrigerator for up to 3 days, or freeze as
soon as cooled, for up to 1 month. Defrost thoroughly, and heat through fully before serving.

Makes 6–8 portions

first fish supper

see variations page 148

Fish is a good source of protein, high in vitamins and minerals and quick to cook. Begin with white fish which is mild in flavour such as flounder, lemon sole, cod and haddock, and gradually introduce stronger-tasting oily fish such as salmon, mackerel and tuna. Oily fish contains high levels of mercury, so you should limit your baby's diet to one serving per week. Make sure that all the bones are removed, to avoid choking hazard.

2 boneless flounder fillets
450 ml (16 fl. oz) or more of milk (use breast
    milk or formula for babies under 12 months)
pinch of dried dill and parsley

2 carrots, peeled and chopped
2 potatoes, peeled and chopped
4 tbsp finely grated Cheddar cheese

Preheat the oven to 190°C (375°F/Gas mark 5). Place the fish fillets in a shallow ovenproof dish, pour over the milk and sprinkle with the herbs. Cover with kitchen foil and bake for 20–25 minutes, until the fish is cooked.

Bring a saucepan of water to a boil, add the carrot and potato and boil for 15 minutes until tender. When the fish is cooked, remove it from the dish and remove the skin. Mash the fish with a little of the milk from the dish. Drain the vegetables and mash them with a little of the milk. Add the grated cheese and mix in. Serve the fish with the mashed cheesy potato and carrot.

Store in the refrigerator for 2 days, or in the freezer for up to 1 month. Freeze as soon as the dish cools, defrost thoroughly and heat through fully before serving.

Makes 4–6 portions

fishcakes

see variations page 149

Fish cakes prepared at home are much healthier than ready-made ones. These are particularly healthy because they're baked in the oven instead of fried. Serve with cooked vegetables such as broccoli, chopped up for babies younger than 12 months.

2 large potatoes, peeled and chopped
2 small skinless white fish fillet – cod, haddock, plaice
900 ml (32 fl. oz) milk (use breast milk or formula for babies under 12 months)

2 knobs of butter
4 eggs, beaten
275 g (10 oz) flour
150 g (6 oz) breadcrumbs

Preheat the oven to 175°C (350°F/Gas mark 4). Boil the potatoes in a saucepan for 15–20 minutes, until soft. Meanwhile, place the fillet in an ovenproof dish, cover with milk and bake for 10–15 minutes, until the fish is cooked through. Remove from the oven and flake the fish, removing all bones. Drain the potatoes and mash with the butter. Add the fish and enough egg to bind the mixture together. You may need only half the egg. Mix well. Form the mixture into balls and flatten them slightly to make small patties. Raise the oven temperature to 200°C (400°F/Gas mark 6). Place the flour in a bowl, the remaining egg in another bowl and the breadcrumbs on a plate. Coat each fishcake in flour, dunk in the egg and finally in the breadcrumbs. Lay the fishcakes on a baking tray, brushed with a little oil. Bake for 10–15 minutes, turning over halfway. Serve.

Store in the refrigerator for up to 2 days, or freeze for up to 1 month. Freeze them as soon as they are cool, defrost thoroughly and heat through fully before serving.

Makes 12–15 small fish cakes

chicken nuggets

see variations page 150

Chicken is a great source of protein for your baby. Chicken nuggets can be a healthy meal. These are shallow-fried or oven-baked, so they are low in fat.

2 skinless, boneless chicken breasts
1 egg white

1 tbsp cornflour
1 tbsp sunflower oil

Cut the chicken breast into 4–5 nugget-sized chunks (about 3.5 cm/1½ in). Mix the egg white and cornflour in a small bowl. It will look lumpy at first, but keep stirring until it has a smooth consistency. Dunk each chicken piece into the egg white and cornflour mixture to coat.

To shallow-fry the nuggets, heat the oil in a non-stick frying over medium heat, then put the nuggets into the hot oil. Fry until golden brown, then turn and cook the other side. Make sure that the chicken is cooked through. If the outside of the chicken cooks too quickly, turn the heat down a little. To oven-bake the nuggets, preheat the oven to 200°C (400°F/Gas mark 6). Put the nuggets on a greased baking tray. Cook for 10–15 minutes, turning halfway, until cooked through and golden brown. Serve with green vegetables, potato wedges and homemade tomato sauce (page 69).

Store in the refrigerator for up to 2 days, or freeze for up to 1 month. Freeze as soon as they are cool, defrost thoroughly and heat through fully before serving.

Makes 8–10 nuggets

beef stroganoff

see variations page 151

This classic Russian dish is quick and easy to make. Not only is it good for babies, it is also delicious as a dinner party dish. Serve with rice, puréed for babies under 9 months.

450 g (1 lb) lean steak	2 tsp olive oil
1 onion	100 ml (4 fl. oz) soured cream
1 tbsp butter	100 g (4 oz) rice

Thinly slice the steak. Peel and chop the onion. Melt the butter and olive oil together in a non-stick frying pan over low heat. Add the onions and allow them to 'sweat' for 10 minutes until softened and translucent; you don't want them to brown.

Add the steak, turn up the heat to medium–high and stir-fry for 3–4 minutes, until the steak is cooked. Add the soured cream and cook for another minute until heated through.

Meanwhile, bring a saucepan of water to the boil. Add the rice and cook according to packet instructions. Drain and serve with the beef and sauce on top.

Discard any uneaten rice immediately. Store the stroganoff in the refrigerator for up to 2 days, or extra portions can be frozen for up to 1 month. Freeze as soon as they are cool, defrost thoroughly and heat through fully before serving.

Makes 6 child portions or 2 adult portions

chilli con carne

see variations page 152

Classic chilli con carne, with the 'chilli' optional for little people. Make for the whole family and serve with a jar of hot chilli sauce on the side. Purée for babies under 9 months as beans could be a choking hazard. Serve with rice (puréed for younger babies), tortilla chips (page 169) or sweet potato wedges (page 146).

1 onion, peeled and finely chopped
1 carrot, peeled and finely chopped
1 tbsp sunflower oil
450 g (1 lb) lean minced beef
1 (215-g/7-oz.) tin kidney beans, drained
   and rinsed

1 (400-g/14-oz.) tin chopped tomatoes
225 ml (8 fl. oz) low-sodium beef stock
½ tsp ground coriander
½ tsp ground cumin
pinch chilli powder (optional)

Heat the oil in a non-stick frying pan over medium heat. Sauté the onion and carrot for 5 minutes, until softened and starting to brown. Transfer to a large saucepan. Break up the minced beef and add to the frying pan. Cook for 4–5 minutes, stirring to break up the meat into tiny pieces, until slightly browned. Transfer to the saucepan.

Place the saucepan over medium heat. Add the beans, tomatoes with their juices, stock, coriander, cumin and chilli powder. Stir to mix well. Bring to the boil, reduce to a simmer, cover and cook for 30–40 minutes, until the meat is cooked and the vegetables are soft.

Store in the refrigerator for up to 2 days, or in the freezer for up to 1 month. Freeze as soon as the dish cools, defrost thoroughly and heat through fully before serving.

Makes 8–10 child portions or 4 adult portions

meatloaf

see variations page 153

A classic meatloaf dish that can be crumbled for baby or sliced as a finger food for a toddler.
It's an all-round family favourite.

1 onion, peeled & grated
1 carrot, peeled & grated
100 g (4 oz) baby spinach, finely chopped
275 g (10 oz) lean minced beef
½ tsp dried herbs of your choice
pinch ground cinnamon

225 g (8 oz) breadcrumbs
4 tbsp grated mozzarella cheese
100 ml (4 fl. oz) milk (use breast milk or
    formula for babies under 12 months)
1 egg

Preheat the oven to 175°C (350°F/Gas mark 4). In a large bowl, mix all the ingredients
together and press into a greased loaf tin. Bake for 1–1¼ hours until cooked through.
Serve warm.

Store in the refrigerator for up to 2 days, or freeze for up to 1 month. Freeze the meatloaf as
soon as it is cool, defrost thoroughly and heat through fully before serving. When reheating,
make sure that the centre of the meatloaf is hot before serving.

Makes 6–8 child portions or 3–4 adult portions

breadsticks

see variations page 154

This basic bread recipe makes healthy, crunchy breadsticks as well as focaccia (page 215) and a base for pizza (page 211).

275 g (10 oz) bread flour, plus a little extra
½ tsp salt
½ tsp sugar

1 tbsp olive oil
1 tsp quick-rising yeast
175 ml (6 fl. oz) warm water

Place the 275 g (10 oz) of flour, salt, sugar, oil and yeast in a large bowl, and mix together. Make a well in the centre of the flour, pour in half the warm water, and combine with your fingers. Add more water gradually until the mixture forms a dough that is soft and slightly sticky.

Dust a clean work surface with a little flour and tip the dough onto it. Sprinkle the dough and your hands with a little flour too. Transfer the dough to a floured surface and knead for 5–10 minutes until smooth and elastic. Replace in the bowl, cover with clingfilm or a damp tea towel and leave in a warm place until it has doubled in size, about 1 hour.

Preheat the oven to 220°C (425°F/Gas mark 7). Knock the dough back (press out any air bubbles) and break off balls of dough. Roll them into long stick shapes (the width of a pencil and about half as long). Transfer the breadsticks to a greased baking tray and bake for 10–15 minutes until golden brown. Transfer to a cooling rack to cool. Once cooled, store the breadsticks in an airtight container; they will keep for up to 3 days. Or freeze for up to 1 month.

Makes 8 breadsticks

dried apple rings

see variations page 155

This is a great recipe if you have your own apple tree or if you can buy apples in bulk when they are in season. Soaking apple slices in the lemon juice prevents them from oxidizing and turning brown. The long, slow cooking process dries out the apples. By removing the water, the apples are preserved, enabling them to keep much longer than fresh apples. Dried apple rings are ideal for babies 9 months old and up to use for teething, and they make a great finger food for toddlers.

10 apples
2 tbsp lemon juice
680 ml (24 fl. oz) water

Peel, core and slice the apples into 5-mm (¼-in) thick rings. Combine the lemon juice and water in a bowl. Put the apples into the mixture for 5 minutes, making sure the apples are completely covered. Drain and pat dry.

Preheat the oven to its lowest setting, around 140°C (275°F/Gas mark 1). Lay the apple slices on wire racks or directly on the oven rack. Be certain the racks are very clean. Bake for 1 hour. Check periodically that the apples aren't burning; you want to dry them out rather than cook them. If they start to brown or look like they are cooking rather than drying, turn off the oven and leave them in the oven for 4–5 hours, until they are dry.

When the apples are dry, remove them from the oven and allow to cool completely. Store in an airtight container for up to 1 month.

Makes 60–70 apple rings

egg-free vanilla ice cream

see variations page 156

Unlike the classic ice cream made with an egg custard base (page 236), this egg-free version of ice cream is just cream and vanilla extract, churned and frozen. Give this only occasionally to your baby as a treat, so that they do not develop a sweet tooth.

450 ml (16 fl. oz) double cream
225 ml (8 fl. oz) milk (use breast milk or
   formula for babies under 12 months)

190 g granulated sugar (optional)
2–3 tsp vanilla extract

Mix all the ingredients together.

To freeze with an ice cream maker: follow the manufacturer's instructions, then transfer to a freezer container and set in the freezer for 30 minutes to firm up before serving.

To freeze without an ice cream maker: pour the mixture into a suitable freezer container and transfer to the freezer. After 1 hour, remove the container, pour the contents into a bowl and whisk to break down the ice crystals. This step is necessary so that you end up with smooth ice cream. Pour the mixture back into the freezer container and freeze. Repeat every hour for the next 4 hours, then the ice cream will be ready to serve.

Store in the freezer for no longer than 1 week. Put the container in the refrigerator 30 minutes before you wish to eat it, as it will be very hard.

Makes 850 ml (1 ¹/₂ pints)

blueberry jelly

see variations page 157

Instead of buying a packet of jelly, make your own with real fruit juice and fruit so children are eating food that is good for them as well as being great fun.

900 g (2 lb) fresh/thawed frozen blueberries
    (including juice)
juice of 2 lemons

1 litre (1¾ pints) water
1 packet unflavoured gelatine

Place 450 g (1 lb) of the blueberries in a saucepan with the lemon juice and 100 ml (4 fl. oz) water. Slowly bring to a simmer, then simmer for 5 minutes until the blueberries collapse. Strain through a fine sieve to remove all the seeds.

Put 900 ml (32 fl. oz) of water into a small bowl, sprinkle in the gelatine and leave to soak for 2 minutes, then set it over a bowl of hot water to melt.

Pour the dissolved gelatine into the blueberry juice and stir in the rest of the water.

Place the remaining blueberries in the bottom of individual dishes, moulds or in a large bowl. Pour the liquid over the blueberries gently, and leave to set in the refrigerator for 2–3 hours.

Store in the refrigerator for up to 3 days. Do not freeze.

Makes 4–6 small desserts or 1 adult one

homemade smoothie popsicles

see variations page 158

Basically frozen smoothies, with all the goodness of fresh fruit. Everyone loves these! Don't forget that honey is not safe for babies under 12 months.

4 navel oranges
1 very ripe mango

1 banana
2 tbsp natural yoghurt

Juice the oranges, removing the seeds. Peel, pit and chop the mango. Peel the banana and chop.

Place the orange juice, mango and banana pieces, yoghurt and honey (if using) into a blender. Purée until smooth. Add a little more orange juice or pineapple juice if the mixture is very thick. Pour into ice lolly or similar moulds and freeze overnight.

Store in the freezer for up to 1 month.

Makes 5–6 popsicles

apple crumble

see variations page 159

A classic dessert that will appeal to all ages, this recipe will make enough for the whole family, and is just as good the second day. It is delicious served with cream, ice cream or custard (serve plain for baby).

275 g (10 oz) self-raising flour
100 g (4 oz) butter or margarine
50 g (2 oz) light brown sugar

700 g (1½ lb) apples, washed, peeled, cored and chopped

Preheat the oven to 200°C (400°F / Gas mark 6). Lightly grease an ovenproof baking dish, about 20 or 23 cm (8 or 9 in) in diameter.

With your fingertips, rub in the flour and butter until it resembles breadcrumbs. Stir in the brown sugar.

Layer the apples in the prepared baking dish. Spoon the crumble mixture over the apples and bake for 20–25 minutes, until the crumble topping is golden brown and the apples are soft. For a baby under 12 months, mash the cooked apples a little before serving. Serve warm or cold.

Store in the refrigerator for up to 3 days or in the freezer for up to 1 month. After freezing, heat through fully before serving.

Makes 8–10 child portions or 4 adult portions

variations

potato farls

see base recipe page 109

wholemeal potato farls
Prepare the basic recipe, replacing the plain flour with wholemeal flour.

sweet potato farls
Prepare the basic recipe, replacing the mashed potatoes with the same amount
of mashed sweet potatoes.

potato farls toasted with butter
Prepare the basic recipe. Just before serving, lightly toast the farls under the grill
or in a toaster, and serve buttered.

mini potato farls
Prepare the basic recipe, but instead of rolling into one circle, roll up small
pieces of the potato mixture into golfball-size balls, flatten and then cook
as before.

parmesan potato farls
Prepare the basic recipe, adding 50 g (2 oz) finely grated Parmesan cheese to
the mixture.

biscotti with babyccino

see base recipe page 111

orange biscotti
Prepare the basic recipe, adding the finely grated zest of 2 oranges to the dry ingredients.

orange & chocolate chip biscotti
Prepare the basic recipe, adding the finely grated zest of 2 oranges to the dry ingredients along with 100 g (4 oz) dark chocolate chips.

cinnamon–raisin biscotti
Prepare the basic recipe, adding 100 g (4 oz) raisins and an additional ½ teaspoon ground cinnamon to the dry ingredients.

apricot–orange biscotti
Prepare the basic recipe, adding the finely grated zest of 2 oranges to the dry ingredients, along with 3–4 finely chopped dried apricots.

variations

baby crêpes

see base recipe page 112

crêpes with apple & cinnamon
Prepare the basic recipe. Before serving, spread 1 tablespoon apple purée (page 30) over the crêpe, and sprinkle with a pinch of ground cinnamon.

crêpes with apple-apricot purée
Prepare the basic recipe. Chop 2 dried apricots and place in a saucepan with 50 ml (2 fl. oz) apple juice. Simmer for 5 minutes until the apricot is soft, mash and serve on top of the crêpes.

crêpes with mashed banana
Prepare the basic recipe. Mash ¼–½ banana and spread over the crêpe before serving.

crêpes with bananas and whipped cream
Prepare the basic recipe. Slice ¼ banana thinly. Top each crêpe with a few banana slices and 1 tablespoon whipped cream. Fold the crêpe over and slice for a delicious treat.

wholemeal & oatmeal crêpes (12 months +)
Prepare the basic recipe, but increase the crêpes' fibre content (once the baby is 12 months old) by replacing the plain flour with 75 g (3 oz) wholemeal flour and 25 g (1 oz) quick-cooking porridge oats.

variations

cheesy mash

see base recipe page 115

cheesy mash with salmon
Prepare the basic recipe, adding a half fillet of cooked salmon, making sure you remove all the skin and bones, into the cheesy mash.

cheesy mash with chicken
Prepare the basic recipe, then shred or chop half a cooked chicken breast into the cheesy mash.

cheesy mash with leeks
Prepare the basic recipe, wash and chop ½ a leek, steam for 8–10 minutes until soft and mix with the mash.

orange cheesy mash
Prepare the basic recipe, adding 1 small, cooked carrot to the potato and mash together with the cheese.

cheesy mash with broccoli
Prepare the basic recipe. Wash and steam 4–5 florets of broccoli for 5–6 minutes until soft, then mash with the cheesy mash until it turns speckled with green bits.

variations

oven-baked potato wedges

see base recipe page 116

oven-baked sweet potato wedges
Prepare the basic recipe, replacing the potato with a sweet potato.
Reduce the cooking time by 5 minutes.

oven-baked carrot slices
Prepare the basic recipe, replacing the potato with 1 large carrot, peeled
and sliced.

oven-baked parsnip slices
Prepare the basic recipe, replacing the potato with 1 parsnip, peeled
and sliced.

oven-baked beetroot slices
Prepare the basic recipe, replacing the potato with 1 beetroot, peeled
and sliced.

oven-baked aubergine slices
Prepare the basic recipe, replacing the potato with 1 aubergine, peeled
and sliced. Reduce the cooking time by 5 minutes.

variations

dhal

see base recipe page 119

sweet potato dhal
Prepare the basic recipe, adding 1 washed, peeled and chopped sweet potato at the same time you add the stock.

carrot & coriander dhal
Prepare the basic recipe, adding 1 washed, peeled and chopped carrot to the dhal when you add the stock. Add 1 teaspoon finely chopped fresh coriander just before the end of the cooking time.

chicken dhal
Prepare the basic recipe, adding 1 skinned, chopped chicken breast to the pan at the same time as the spices.

turkey & carrot dhal
Prepare the basic recipe, adding 50 g (2 oz) minced turkey to the pan at the same time as the spices. Add 1 washed, peeled and chopped carrot when you add the stock.

dhal with cod (or other white fish)
Prepare the basic recipe, adding 1 skinned, deboned and chopped white fish fillet when you add the stock.

variations

first fish supper

see base recipe page 121

first fish supper with peas
Prepare the basic recipe, omitting the carrots and adding 1 tablespoon fresh or frozen peas to the potato 5 minutes before the end of the cooking time. Purée the peas with the potato. This will make a sweet green mash.

first fish supper with broccoli
Prepare the basic recipe, adding 4 broccoli florets to steam on top of the potato and carrot for 10 minutes, until tender.

first fish supper with beetroot
Prepare the basic recipe, but replace the carrot with 1 washed, peeled and chopped beetroot. This makes a lovely pink mash.

first fish & salmon supper
Prepare the basic recipe, adding ½ boneless salmon fillet to the white fish. If baby likes it, then next time replace the white fish with salmon.

first fish supper with sweet potato
Prepare the basic recipe, replacing the potatoes with 2 large sweet potatoes.

variations

fishcakes

see base recipe page 122

fish and sweet potato cakes
Prepare the basic recipe, replacing the potatoes with 2 large sweet potatoes.

fish cakes with pea purée
Prepare the basic recipe. Steam 2 tablespoons peas. When tender, mash with
a little crème fraîche and add to the mashed potato.

fish and carrot cakes
Prepare the basic recipe, replacing 1 potato with 2 large carrots. Peel and chop
the carrots, boil them in a saucepan with the potatoes, until soft. Mash with
the potato and butter, and prepare as before.

salmon cakes
Prepare the basic recipe, adding ½ boneless salmon fillet to the white fish.
If baby likes it, then next time replace the white fish with salmon.

tuna cakes
Prepare the basic recipe, adding 60 g (2½ oz) tinned tuna in spring water,
drained. If baby likes it, then next time replace the white fish with tuna.

variations

chicken nuggets

see base recipe page 124

herby chicken nuggets
Prepare the basic recipe, adding 1 teaspoon dried tarragon or other herbs of your choice, to the egg white and cornflour mixture.

chicken nuggets with breadcrumbs
Prepare the basic recipe, replacing the egg white and cornflour with 1 whole egg, well beaten. After dunking the nuggets into the egg, coat both sides with dried breadcrumbs before cooking.

chicken nuggets with cornmeal
Prepare the basic recipe, replacing the egg white and cornflour with 1 whole egg, well beaten. After dunking the nuggets into the egg, coat both sides with cornmeal, before cooking.

chicken nuggets with crushed chips (12 months +)
Prepare the basic recipe, replacing the egg white and cornflour with 1 whole egg, well beaten. After dunking the nuggets into the egg, coat both sides with finely crushed unsalted potato chips, before cooking.

beef stroganoff

see base recipe page 125

chicken stroganoff
Prepare basic recipe, replacing the beef with 1 chopped skinless and boneless chicken breast.

creamy beef stroganoff
Prepare basic recipe, replacing the soured cream with single cream for a richer version.

beef & mushroom stroganoff
Prepare basic recipe, adding 100 g (4 oz) sliced mushrooms when you start to cook the steak.

beef stroganoff with mashed potatoes
Prepare basic recipe, replacing the rice with mashed potatoes.

beef stroganoff with noodles
Prepare basic recipe, replacing the rice with noodles such as tagliatelle.

lentil stroganoff
Prepare the basic recipe, replacing the beef with 200 g (7 oz) red lentils. In a saucepan, cook the lentils for 20 minutes until tender, and prepare as before.

variations

chilli con carne

see base recipe page 126

lamb chilli con carne
Prepare the basic recipe, replacing the minced beef with minced lamb.

turkey chilli con carne
Prepare the basic recipe, replacing the minced beef with minced turkey.

vegetable chilli
Prepare the basic recipe, replacing the beef stock with vegetable stock, and the minced beef with 1 chopped courgette, 1 chopped aubergine, and 225 g (8 oz) chopped mushrooms.

three-bean chilli
Prepare the basic recipe, replacing the minced beef with 450 g (1 lb) of different tinned beans such as pinto beans, chickpeas or black beans.

chilli con carne with cheesy garlic bread (12 months +)
Prepare the basic recipe. Thinly slice some bread, brush with a little olive oil and rub with a peeled garlic clove. Sprinkle half a tablespoon of grated mozzarella cheese onto the bread, and toast under the grill. Serve the chilli on the toasted bread, or with the bread on the side.

variations

meatloaf

see base recipe page 129

turkey loaf
Prepare the basic recipe, replacing the minced beef with minced turkey.

chicken loaf
Prepare the basic recipe, replacing the minced beef with minced chicken.

lamb loaf
Prepare the basic recipe, replacing the minced beef with minced lamb.

vegetable loaf
Prepare the basic recipe, replacing the minced beef with 200 g (7 oz) red lentils
and adding 100 g (4 oz) tinned chopped tomatoes, drained. In a saucepan,
cook the lentils, chopped tomatoes and milk for 20 minutes, until the lentils
are tender. Mix with the remaining ingredients and bake for 30–45 minutes,
until the top of the loaf looks dry.

variations

breadsticks

see base recipe page 130

bread rolls
Prepare the basic recipe, but split the dough into 6 pieces, roll into balls and bake as for breadsticks.

wholemeal breadsticks
Prepare the basic recipe, replacing half the bread flour with wholemeal flour.

poppy seed breadsticks (12 months +)
Prepare the basic recipe. Before baking, sprinkle waxed paper with 2 tablespoons poppy seeds. Roll the breadsticks in the seeds before baking.

parmesan breadsticks (12 months +)
Prepare the basic recipe, adding 2 tablespoons finely grated Parmesan cheese to the dry ingredients.

variations

dried apple rings

see base recipe page 132

dried apple rings with cinnamon
Prepare the basic recipe, sprinkling the apple slices with a little ground
cinnamon before putting them into the oven.

dried pear slices
Prepare the basic recipe, replacing the apples with peeled, halved, cored and
sliced pears. If you want, sprinkle them with a little ground ginger before
putting them into the oven.

dried peach or plum slices
Prepare the basic recipe, replacing the apples with peeled, halved, pitted
and sliced peaches or plums. If you want, sprinkle them with a little ground
cinnamon before putting them into the oven.

dried apple rings with ricotta cheese
Prepare the basic recipe. To serve, slice the dried rings in half. Serve with
1 tablespoon ricotta cheese as a dip.

rehydrated with sultanas & yoghurt (12 months +)
Prepare the basic recipe. Soak the apple rings in water or apple juice for
20–30 minutes, drain and serve with sultanas and yoghurt.

variations

egg-free vanilla ice-cream

see base recipe page 134

egg-free strawberry ice cream (12 months +)
Prepare the basic recipe, reducing the cream to 275 ml (10 fl. oz) and omitting
the milk and vanilla. Wash, hull and purée 450 g (1 lb) strawberries. Push
through a sieve to remove the seeds, mix with the cream and sugar and freeze.

egg-free blueberry ice cream
Prepare the basic recipe, reducing the cream to 275 ml (10 fl. oz) and omitting
the milk and vanilla. Wash, hull and purée 450 g (1 lb) blueberries. Push through
a sieve to remove any seeds, mix with the cream and sugar and freeze.

egg-free chocolate ice cream (12 months +)
Prepare the basic recipe, omitting the vanilla and reducing the cream to 175 ml
(6 fl. oz). Warm the milk and cream, and add 150 g (5 oz) chocolate chips. Stir to
melt the chocolate, add the sugar, chill and freeze.

egg-free banana ice cream
Prepare the basic recipe, reducing the cream to 275 ml (10 fl. oz). Purée 2 ripe
bananas with the milk, mix with the cream and sugar and freeze.

egg-free marbled ice cream (12 months +)
Prepare the basic recipe and the Apple and Mango Sorbet (page 84). Stir the ice
cream and sorbet together, creating a ripple effect, then put in the freezer.

blueberry jelly

see base recipe page 137

orange jelly (12 months +)
Prepare the basic recipe, omitting the blueberries and the lemon juice. Remove the skin and pith from 1 orange and split it into segments. Put the orange pieces in the bottom of the dishes. Reduce the water to 175 ml (6 fl. oz) and add 175 ml (6 fl. oz) orange juice, freshly squeezed from 5 or 6 oranges.

creamy blueberry jelly
Prepare the basic recipe, replacing 175 ml (6 fl. oz) of the water with 175 ml (6 fl. oz) single cream once the gelatine has been added.

strawberry jelly with summer fruit (12 months +)
Prepare the basic recipe, replacing the blueberries with fresh or thawed frozen strawberries, and adding a handful of summer berries to the glasses or mould.

summer berry jelly (12 months +)
Prepare the basic recipe, replacing the blueberries with the same quantity of summer berries fresh or thawed frozen, such as blackberries, strawberries and raspberries.

variations

homemade smoothie popsicle

see base recipe page 138

frozen vanilla smoothie popsicle
Prepare the basic recipe. Replace the plain yoghurt with vanilla yoghurt.

frozen blueberry smoothie popsicle
Prepare the basic recipe, replacing the mango with 400 g (14 oz) fresh or thawed frozen blueberries. Purée the berries, then push through a fine-mesh strainer to remove the seeds before mixing with the other ingredients.

frozen tropical fruit smoothie popsicle
Prepare the basic recipe, adding 1 very ripe small pineapple, peeled, cored and chopped, and 1 passion fruit, halved, flesh scooped out, and sieved to remove seeds. Add 2 extra tablespoons yoghurt. You will make about 10–12 popsicles.

frozen strawberry smoothie popsicle (12 months +)
Prepare the basic recipe, replacing the mango with 200 g (7 oz) very ripe strawberries. Purée the berries, then push through a fine-mesh strainer to remove the seeds before mixing with the other ingredients.

frozen mango–raspberry smoothie popsicle (12 months +)
Prepare the basic recipe, adding 200 g (7 oz) raspberries to the mango. Purée the berries, then pour through a fine-mesh strainer to remove the seeds before mixing with the other ingredients.

apple crumble

see base recipe page 140

apple & pear crumble
Prepare the basic recipe, replacing half the apples with peeled and chopped pears.

apple & rhubarb crumble
Prepare the basic recipe, replacing half the apples with 225 g (8 oz) chopped rhubarb.

apple & apricot crumble
Prepare the basic recipe, replacing half the apples with 6 pitted and chopped fresh apricots.

apple & blueberry crumble
Prepare the basic recipe, replacing half the apples with 400 g (14 oz) fresh or thawed frozen blueberries.

peach crumble
Prepare the basic recipe, replacing half the apples with 3 peeled, pitted and chopped fresh peaches.

toddler foods: 12 months +

Now's the time to let your little one help with the cooking. If they can stand unaided and hold a spoon, they can assist you! Toddlers love stirring — give them their own bowl to copy you, and introduce them to a skill that will last them a lifetime — cooking.

breakfast muffins

see variations page 239

The wholemeal flour used in this recipe contains more fibre than white flour. This fibre helps keep children fuller for longer and also helps stave off sugar cravings.

150 g (5 oz) wholemeal flour
75 g (3 oz) plain flour
2 tsp baking powder
1 tsp ground cinnamon
1 tsp ground ginger
175 g (6 oz) dark brown sugar

3 carrots, peeled and grated
1 apple, peeled, cored and grated
1 egg
175 ml (6 fl. oz) milk
175 ml (6 fl. oz) sunflower oil

Preheat the oven to 175°C (350°F/Gas mark 4). Prepare a regular-size muffin tin or a mini-muffin tin with paper baking cups or by greasing the pan. Mix together the flour, baking powder, spices and sugar. Add the grated carrots and apple and stir to mix.

In a separate bowl, beat the egg, add the milk and sunflower oil and beat well. Pour mixture into the dry ingredients. Mix well; don't worry if there are any lumps as they will even out during cooking. Evenly fill the muffin cups. Bake regular-size muffins for 15–20 minutes until golden and firm to the touch (10–15 minutes for mini muffins). When a toothpick inserted in the centre of a muffin comes out clean, remove the pan from the oven. Allow muffins to cool before removing from pan.

Store in an airtight container for up to 3 days, or freeze immediately and use within 1 month. To use from frozen, carefully defrost and heat through fully before serving.

Makes 12 regular or 24 mini muffins

bircher muesli

see variations page 240

Make this traditional Swiss muesli for the whole family. This recipe makes 1 adult serving. For babies between 6 and 9 months, purée it in the food processor.

2 tbsp quick-cooking porridge oats
a little apple juice (preferably made from
    fresh apples)

1 apple
1 tbsp full-fat natural yoghurt

Soak the oats in a little apple juice, just enough to thoroughly moisten them. Leave to soak for at least 1 hour or overnight.

Wash, peel, core and grate the apple. Stir pieces through the oats, then stir in the yoghurt. Purée if required.

Store in the refrigerator for up to 3 days.

Makes 2–4 portions

granola bars

see variations page 241

These healthy bars are packed full of dried fruit, nuts and seeds. Do not give these to a baby under 12 months (the maple syrup is not safe for them). These bars are delicious without the nuts, so simply omit for a child with a nut allergy.

6 tbsp butter, plus extra for greasing
3 tbsp maple syrup
3 tbsp fruit spread (such as pear or apricot)
100 g (4 oz) light brown sugar
275 g (10 g) old-fashioned porridge oats
   (not quick-cooking oats)

2 tbsp pecan halves
50 g (2 oz) golden raisins
4 tbsp mixed seeds, such as sunflower,
   pumpkin, flax, sesame
2 tbsp ground almonds

Preheat the oven to 175°C (350°F/Gas mark 4). Grease a 20-cm (8-in) square cake pan with a little butter and line it with waxed or parchment paper. Place the butter, maple syrup, fruit spread and sugar in a saucepan over medium heat. Heat until the butter has melted and the sugar has dissolved. Stir well to mix. Bring to the boil and cook for 2 minutes until it has a thick, sticky consistency.

Place the remaining ingredients in a large bowl. Pour in the melted ingredients and mix well. Pour into the prepared cake pan, flatten with a wooden spoon and bake for 15–20 minutes until golden brown. Remove from the oven and leave to cool. Cut into squares. Keep in an airtight container for 3–4 days, or freeze extra portions the day they are made for up to 1 month. If freezing, defrost thoroughly, allow to come to room temperature, and serve.

Makes 12–16 bars

cream cheese pinwheels

see variations page 242

Although these can be described as painstaking, the result is usually met by squeals of joy from babies and toddlers, so the effort is worth it.

1 slice thin-sliced bread (or 1 wrap)
cream cheese

If you are using sliced bread, cut off the crusts. Spread a thin layer of cream cheese on one side of the bread or wrap. Roll up tightly so it looks like a log and secure with a toothpick.

Use a sharp knife to cut 1-cm (½-in) wide slices from the log. When you turn them on their side, you will see the 'pinwheel' effect. Remove the toothpick. Serve immediately, or double-wrap in clingfilm and refrigerate no longer than 24 hours to prevent pinwheels from drying out.

Makes one portion

butter bean dip with tortilla chips

see variations page 243

Butter beans are a good source of protein, fibre and magnesium. They can be served as a finger food on their own — just slip off their skins before serving — and they're also good mashed in this lovely dip. Serve in a bowl with tortilla chips. These chips made from tortilla wraps are healthier than ready-made tortilla chips because they are much lower in fat and salt. They're great for small fingers.

1 (225-g/8-oz) tin butter beans, drained and
    rinsed (or 225 g/8 oz frozen butter beans,
    cooked)
1 tbsp extra-virgin olive oil
1 garlic clove, peeled and crushed

1 tbsp full-fat natural yoghurt
pinch ground cumin
1 tbsp washed and chopped fresh flat-leaf
    parsley
1 tortilla, white or wholemeal

To make the dip: put all the ingredients in a blender or food processor and blend until smooth. Add a little more yoghurt or olive oil to achieve a smooth purée. Store in the refrigerator for up to 3 days.

To make the tortilla chips: heat a frying pan until it is hot, add the tortilla, and cook for 3–4 minutes on each side until it is golden brown and crispy. Remove from heat, break into pieces, allow to cool for few minutes and serve on their own or with the butter bean dip.

Makes 4–5 servings of lima dip for every tortilla serving

tahini dip

see variations page 244

Please note — tahini is made from ground sesame seeds and is not suitable for people suffering from sesame seed allergy. Tahini is a key ingredient in hummus, but it makes a lovely dip on its own. It is especially good with oven-baked potato, aubergine and courgette wedges (pages 116 and 146).

1 tbsp tahini paste
3–4 tbsp water

Mix the tahini and water together. If it seems a little thick, add a little more water. It can be kept in the refrigerator for 3–4 days.

Makes 4 portions

baby guacamole

see variations page 245

A very easy dip made from a fresh avocado. For younger babies, purée it. For older babies, mash the avocado with a fork. If you make it in advance, quickly cover the bowl with a double layer of clingfilm to delay the guacamole from turning brown. Because there is lemon juice in the dip, it is not suitable for babies under 12 months. For adults, you may want to add some chilli powder or paprika to enhance the flavour.

1 ripe avocado
juice of ½ lemon

Halve the avocado, remove the stone and scoop out the flesh. Purée or mash with the lemon juice and serve with finger foods such as breadsticks (page 130), tortilla chips (page 169) or vegetable sticks such as cucumber and carrot.

Store in the refrigerator for up to 24 hours. The avocado will eventually turn brown because it oxidixes when it is exposed to air. This will not affect the flavour, however, and the surface can be scraped off easily.

Makes 4 portions

hummus

see variations page 246

Originating in the Middle East, hummus is a dip made from puréed chickpeas. This recipe used tinned chickpeas. If you prefer to use dried chickpeas, follow the instructions on the bag precisely, as undercooked beans can be dangerous. If your baby is under 12 months, do not use the tahini. Serve with vegetable sticks, pita bread strips, tortilla chips (page 169), or breadsticks (page 130).

1 (400-g/14-oz) tin chickpeas, drained and
    rinsed
1 tbsp extra-virgin olive oil
1 garlic clove, peeled and crushed

3 tbsp full-fat natural yoghurt
1 tbsp tahini paste (optional; omit for
    sesame seed allergies or for babies
    under 12 months)

Place all the ingredients in a blender or food processor. Blend until smooth, adding a little more yoghurt or olive oil if needed to achieve a smooth purée. Hummus can be stored in an airtight container in the refrigerator for up to 3 days.

Makes 4 servings

mackerel pâté

see variations page 247

Pre-prepared smoked mackerel fillets make this a quick and easy pâté. Make sure you remove all the bones and the skin. Mackerel is an oily fish that could contain mercury. Therefore we recommend you feed a baby (over 12 months) this recipe and other dishes containing oily fish only on an occasional basis. Despite the mercury content, it's important to remember that oily fish contains many wonderful nutrients for your baby, so it is good that they develop a taste for it. If you wish to make it for adults too, use one fillet per person.

1 mackerel fillet, all bones removed
40g (1½ oz) cream cheese
1 tsp finely chopped fresh chives

pinch cayenne pepper
grated zest and juice of ¼ lemon

Flake the mackerel, add the rest of the ingredients and purée. Cover and refrigerate. Will keep for up to 3 days in the refrigerator.

Makes 2 portions

oatcakes

see variations page 248

These small savoury biscuits are ideal for little fingers. These are good as a savoury baby biscuit or rusk for teething babies, and are lovely with dips too. They are equally good for adults to eat with cheese.

350 g (13 oz) porridge oats
¼ tsp bicarbonate of soda

2 tbsp white vegetable fat
275 ml (10 fl. oz) water

Preheat the oven to 175°C (350°F/Gas mark 4). Place the oats in a food processor and process for 30–60 seconds until the oats resemble a coarse flour. Mix together the oats and bicarbonate of soda.

Place the fat in a saucepan with the water. Heat gently until the fat melts. Add enough of the liquid to the oatmeal mixture to make a firm dough.

Transfer the dough to a piece of waxed or parchment paper. Roll out the dough until it is approximately 3 mm (⅛ in) thick. Use a round cutter to cut out circles. Place the oatcakes on a baking tray lined with parchment paper. Bake for 12–15 minutes.

Remove from the oven and transfer to a cooling rack to completely cool. They can be stored in an airtight container for up to 1 week.

Makes 12 oatcakes

roasted red pepper & tomato soup

see variations page 249

When your baby is 12 months or older, try this soup. It can be served hot or cold. It makes a tasty topping for pizza (page 211), and works well as a pasta sauce. If you are making this for the family, increase the quantities 3 or 4 times (for a family of 4–5).

2 red peppers
8 tomatoes
2 red onions

a little olive oil
1.2 litres (2 pints) low-sodium vegetable stock

Preheat the oven to 220°C (425°F/Gas mark 7). Wash the red peppers, cut in half and remove seeds. Cut each half into 3 slices. Wash and halve the tomatoes. Peel the onions and cut into sixths. Lay the peppers, tomatoes and onions on a greased baking tray. Drizzle with a little olive oil.

Transfer the pan to the oven and roast for 30–35 minutes, until the peppers are slightly browned at the edges. Transfer the peppers to a plastic freezer-weight bag, tie the top closed and leave for 5 minutes. The steam from the peppers will make them easy to peel.

Meanwhile, peel the tomatoes and transfer them and the onions to a saucepan with the stock. Untie the bag of peppers and peel off the skin. Add the peppers to the stock. Bring to the boil. Cover and simmer for 30 minutes. Purée.

Freeze extra portions in freezerproof containers, label and use within 3 months. To use from frozen, carefully defrost. Heat through fully before serving.

Makes 12–16 portions

mini-minestrone

see variations page 250

This lovely hearty soup is great for cold weather. You can use any kind of very small pasta. Cut toast fingers or bread fingers to serve with it. They are lovely to dunk into the soup and eat with your fingers. If you are making this for the whole family, increase the quantities 3 or 4 times (for a family of 4–5).

2 onions
2 red peppers
a little olive oil
1 courgette
2 carrots, peeled

1 (400-g/14-oz) tin chopped tomatoes
680 ml (24 fl. oz) low-sodium vegetable
   or chicken stock
75 g (3 oz) very small pasta or spaghetti
   broken into small pieces

Wash, peel and chop the onions and peppers. Heat the oil in a frying pan, add the onion and pepper and sauté over a gentle heat for 6–7 minutes, until soft. Transfer to a saucepan.

Wash and grate the courgette and carrots and add them to the saucepan. Add the stock and tinned tomatoes, with their juice. Bring to the boil. Cover and simmer for 20 minutes.

Return to the pan, add the pasta and cook for a further 10 minutes, until the pasta is soft.

Freeze extra portions in freezer-proof containers, label, and use within 3 months. To use from frozen, carefully defrost. Heat through fully before serving.

Makes 12–16 portions

fish chowder

see variations page 251

Healthy, filling and warming, a fabulous recipe for baby and for the rest of the family. If you are making this for the whole family, double the quantities (for a family of 4–5).

2 fillets of white fish such as cod, haddock or
    plaice, skinned and boned
2 medium potatoes
2 carrots

2 small onions
2 tsp butter
2 tbsp plain flour
900 ml (32 fl. oz) milk

Cut fish into small pieces and check for any additional bones. Wash, peel and chop the potatoes, carrots and onions. If you prefer, you can grate the vegetables instead of dicing, which will give you fewer lumps.

Melt the butter in a frying pan. Add the vegetables and sauté for 5 minutes over low heat. Stir in the flour and mix to coat the vegetables. Pour in half the milk, gradually blending with the floured vegetables. Bring to the boil and simmer for 20–30 minutes, until the potato is tender.

Add the remaining milk and the fish pieces. Continue cooking for 10 minutes more or until the fish is thoroughly cooked. Mash the fish pieces with a fork and serve.

Freeze extra portions in freezerproof containers, label, and use within 3 months. To use from frozen, carefully defrost. Heat through fully before serving.

Makes 6–8 portions

pasta with pea pesto

see variations page 252

All you need to do is cook some fresh or dried pasta, then stir through this lovely creamy sauce to make a fabulous meal. You could serve a bowl of plain cooked pasta to your toddler and give them a spoonful of the sauce for them to mix themselves. For younger babies, use very small pasta shapes and make sure the sauce is well mixed.

275 g (10 oz) frozen peas, cooked
50 ml (2 fl. oz) crème fraîche

25 g (1 oz) fresh mint
finely grated Parmesan, to serve

Place all the ingredients in a food processor or blender and purée. Stir the sauce through hot cooked pasta and serve with finely grated Parmesan sprinkled on top.

The sauce can be refrigerated for up to 3 days, but not frozen. Crème fraîche does not freeze well.

Makes 4 child portions or 2 adult portions

aubergine bake

see variations page 253

This traditional Italian dish is a firm family favourite. The aubergine soaks up the flavours of the tomato and basil, the cheese melts and it is delicious with lots of crusty bread to soak up the juices.

3 small aubergines
3 tbsp olive oil
250 g (9 oz) grated or torn mozzarella
100–325 ml (4–12 fl. oz Classic Tomato Sauce
   (page 69)

3 tbsp chopped fresh basil leaves
6 heaping tbsp grated Parmesan

Preheat the oven to 190°C (375°F/Gas mark 5). Slice the aubergine into 1-cm (½-in) slices. Heat the olive oil in a nonstick frying pan and fry the aubergine until golden brown on both sides. Drain on kitchen towel.

Place half the aubergine slices in a layer in the bottom of a small casserole dish, layer with half the mozzarella, half the tomato sauce, half the basil and half the Parmesan. Repeat, finishing with the Parmesan. Bake for 20–30 minutes, until the cheese is golden brown and the dish is bubbling. Serve with green vegetables or a salad and crusty bread.

Store in the refrigerator for up to 2 days or freeze for up to 1 month. Freeze extra portions in small sealable bags or containers, and label. To use from frozen, carefully defrost. Heat through fully before serving.

Makes 6 portions

veggie korma

see variations page 254

Korma is a mild, creamy curry dish that introduces babies to the flavour of mild spices. Traditionally, this dish includes ground almonds, but I have excluded them from this recipe because of the risk of nut allergies.

1 tbsp sunflower oil
1 (1-cm/½-in) piece root ginger, peeled and
    finely chopped
1 clove garlic, peeled and finely chopped
½ small onion, peeled and finely chopped
½ tsp each ground cumin and coriander
pinch powdered turmeric
1 small potato, peeled and chopped

1 carrot, peeled and chopped
1 tsp tomato paste
100 ml (4 fl. oz) low-sodium vegetable stock
2 tbsp frozen peas
6–8 broccoli florets
100 ml (4 fl. oz) single cream
1 tbsp finely chopped fresh coriander
200 g (7 oz) rice

Heat the oil in a nonstick frying pan. Put the root ginger, garlic and onion in a food processor and blend to a purée, adding 1 tablespoon water if the mixture is very thick. Add mixture to the frying pan and cook on medium–low heat for 5 minutes. Add the spices, and cook for 2–3 minutes. Add the potato and carrot, along with the tomato paste and vegetable stock, reduce to a simmer, cover and cook for 15–20 minutes, until the vegetables are soft.

Stir in the peas and broccoli florets, and cook for 5 minutes. Stir in the cream and coriander and cook for 3–4 minutes. Serve with boiled rice. Store in the refrigerator for up to 3 days or in the freezer for up to 1 month. Freeze extra portions in freezer-proof containers, label and use within 1 month. To use from frozen, carefully defrost. Heat through fully before serving.

Makes 4 child portions or 2 adult portions

macaroni cheese

see variations page 255

This classic childhood dish is a comfort food for toddlers and adults alike. The macaroni is easy for toddlers to pick up with their fingers and great for older toddlers to 'hook' onto forks. To make this for babies under 12 months, use breast milk or formula instead of cow's milk.

2 tbsp butter	40 g (1½ oz) grated Cheddar
2 tbsp flour	100 g (4 oz) macaroni
225 ml (8 fl. oz) milk	2 tbsp finely grated Parmesan

To make the cheese sauce: melt the butter in a saucepan, then add the flour, stirring constantly. Stir for 1–2 minutes to make a smooth roux, then add the milk a little at a time, stirring constantly. Keep adding the milk little by little, making sure it has been absorbed, until the sauce is smooth. When all the milk has been added, stir and gently bring to the boil, which will help thicken the sauce. Just as it reaches the boil, remove the pan from the heat and stir in the grated cheese. Meanwhile, bring a saucepan of water to a boil, add the macaroni and cook for 10–15 minutes until al dente. Drain, then return to the pot.

Pour the cheese sauce over the macaroni, transfer to a heatproof dish, sprinkle with the grated Parmesan, and brown under a hot grill. Serve warm. Mash or purée for babies under 12 months.

Store in the refrigerator for up to 2 days, or freeze extra portions in freezer-proof containers, label and use within 1 month. To use from frozen, carefully defrost. Heat through fully before serving.

Makes 4–6 child portions or 1–2 adult portions

homemade baked beans

see variations page 256

Baked beans are a hugely popular dish, but they can be high in salt and sugar. This homemade version is fabulous, lower in salt and sugar and extremely tasty as well as easy to make. You can vary the beans or use a mixture of different types. Larger beans such as butter beans can be held as a finger food. For younger babies, you may wish to mash the beans a little to make them safer and easier to swallow. Do not add any salt to the recipe or it will make the beans tough.

1 tbsp sunflower oil
1 onion
225 g (8 oz) tinned beans (such as butter or
    small white beans), drained and rinsed
1tsp mustard powder

1tsp black treacle
1 (230-g/8-oz) tin chopped tomatoes
1 tbsp tomato paste
1 tsp dark brown sugar
225 ml (8 fl. oz) low-sodium vegetable stock

Preheat the oven to 140°C (275°F/Gas mark 1). Heat the oil in a heavy ovenproof dish with a lid. Peel and finely chop the onion, add to the oil and cook over low heat for 10–15 minutes, until translucent and soft. Add the remaining ingredients, mix well and bring to the boil. Remove from the heat, cover and transfer to the oven to cook for 4 hours. Stir occasionally while baking.

Store in the refrigerator for up to 3 days, or freeze extra portions in freezerproof containers, label and use within 1 month. To use from frozen, carefully defrost. Heat through fully before serving.

Makes 8 child portions or 4 adult portions

cauliflower cheese

see variations page 257

Making a cheese sauce to go with vegetables is an easy way to tempt children to eat vegetables. A cauliflower is a lot more tasty with a cheese sauce than on its own, and in the UK 'cauliflower cheese' is a popular comfort food. You can adapt the recipe by adding a little hot sauce to spice up the cheese sauce for adults sharing the meal or by sprinkling some grated Parmesan cheese on the top before grilling.

1 cauliflower, washed and broken into florets
1 quantity cheese sauce (page 191)

Steam the cauliflower over boiling water for 10–15 minutes, until tender. Meanwhile, make the cheese sauce.

Drain the cauliflower, transfer to a heatproof baking dish and cover with the sauce. Brown for a few minutes under a hot grill and serve warm. Mash or purée for younger children.

Store in the refrigerator for up to 3 days, or freeze extra portions in freezerproof containers, label and use within 1 month. To use from frozen, carefully defrost. Heat through fully before serving.

Makes 4–6 baby portions or 2–3 adult portions

family fish pie

see variations page 258

Fish cooked in a creamy cheese sauce with mashed potato topping is a great family meal, packed with vitamins and minerals.

450 g (1 lb) firm skinless white fish, such as
    cod, haddock, hake or pollock
225 ml (8 fl. oz) milk
1 bay leaf
1 pinch dried tarragon and parsley

450 g (1 lb) potatoes, peeled and chopped
2 medium carrots, peeled and chopped
1 tsp butter
1 quantity cheese sauce (page 191), using the
    milk from cooking the fish

Preheat the oven to 175°C (350°F/Gas mark 4). Place the fish into a casserole dish. Cover with the milk and add the bay leaf and herbs. Bake for 30–40 minutes, until the fish is cooked through. Place the potatoes and carrots in a pan of water, bring to the boil, and simmer for 15–20 minutes, until soft. Drain and mash with the butter. Set aside.

Remove the fish from the oven and pour the milk into a measuring cup. Add more milk as needed to measure 225 ml (8 fl. oz). Make sure all the bones are removed. Flake the fish and return to the casserole dish. Make the cheese sauce, using the milk from cooking the fish. Pour the cheese sauce over the fish. Place the potato and carrot mash over the top. Smooth down with a fork, sprinkle with a little grated cheese and bake for 30–40 minutes until the potato is golden brown and the fish is heated through. Serve warm.

Store in the refrigerator for up to 2 days, or freeze extra portions in freezer-proof containers, label and use within 1 month. To use from frozen, carefully defrost. Heat through fully before serving.

Makes 6–8 child portions or 2–3 adult portions

fish fingers

see variations page 259

Ready-made fish fingers can be full of additives. If you make them yourself, you know exactly what ingredients have gone into them and you can use the best-quality fish. If you bake them rather than fry, you reduce the amount of fat, making them a lot healthier.

225 g (8 oz) firm white fish such as cod or
    haddock, skin and bones removed
1 tbsp cornflour or plain flour

1 egg, beaten
275 g (10 oz) dried breadcrumbs
1 tbsp sunflower oil

Cut the fish into 8–9 finger-size strips. Place the flour, egg and breadcrumbs in three different shallow bowls and dip each strip of fish into the flour, then the egg and then the breadcrumbs.

To bake: preheat the oven to 200°C (400°F/Gas mark 6). Place the coated fish fingers on a baking tray, brushed with a little oil. Cook for 10–15 minutes, turning over halfway, until cooked through and golden brown. Serve with green vegetables, potato wedges (page 116) and homemade tomato sauce (page 69) or ketchup (page 97).

Store in the refrigerator for up to 2 days, or freeze extra portions in freezer-proof containers, label and use within 1 month. To use from frozen, carefully defrost. Heat through fully before serving.

Makes 8–9 fish sticks

moroccan chicken with couscous

see variations page 260

This chicken dish is great with couscous. This dish is great for the whole family to share; just make sure that the chicken is chopped smaller for toddlers than for the adults.

2 onions, peeled and chopped
1 garlic clove, peeled and chopped
1 tbsp chopped fresh coriander
½ tsp. each ground coriander and cumin
pinch powdered turmeric
juice of 2 lemons
1 tbsp olive oil

2 skinless, boneless chicken breasts
1 tbsp sunflower oil
1 carrot, peeled and chopped
about 225 ml (8 fl. oz) low-sodium chicken
    stock
3 dried apricots, finely chopped
1 tsp honey

To make the marinade, put half the onion, the garlic, herbs and spices, half the lemon juice and the olive oil in a food processor. Blend to a purée. Chop the chicken and add to the marinade. Mix well. Marinate for 4 hours or overnight, making sure that the chicken is covered. To cook, heat the oil in a nonstick frying pan. Add the chicken with the marinade, and cook over medium heat, stirring, to brown the chicken. Add the carrot and the remaining onion to the pan, along with enough chicken stock to cover the ingredients. Add the apricots with the honey and remaining lemon juice to the pan. Bring to a simmer. Cook for 20–30 minutes, uncovered, until the chicken is cooked and the vegetables are soft. Serve.

Store in the refrigerator for up to 2 days. Freeze extra portions in sealable containers, label, and use within 1 month. To use from frozen, carefully defrost. Heat through fully before serving.

Makes 8 child portions or 3–4 adult portions

sweet & sour chicken with rice

see variations page 261

This sweet and sour recipe is very healthy as the meat isn't deep-fried. Serve with rice and vegetables — baby corn, green beans, mushrooms and courgettes all work well.

2 tbsp sunflower oil
4 skinless, boneless chicken breasts, chopped
2 sweet red peppers, chopped
2 medium carrots, chopped
2 (228-g/8-oz) tins pineapple chunks in juice
2 tsp soy sauce

2 tbsp tomato paste
2 tsp sugar
2 tsp rice wine vinegar
2 tsp cornflour
2 tbsp water
200 g (7 oz) rice

Heat the sunflower oil in a wok or large frying pan. Stir-fry the chicken, red pepper and carrot for 5–10 minutes, until the chicken is cooked through and the vegetables are soft.

Cook the rice by placing the rice and water in a small saucepan over medium heat. Bring to the boil, cover and simmer for 10–15 minutes, until the water has been absorbed and the rice is cooked. Pour the pineapple chunks with the juice into a food processor. Add the soy sauce, tomato paste, sugar and vinegar. Blend to a smooth purée. Add mixture to the saucepan and stir to mix well with the chicken and vegetables. Mix the cornflour with the water until smooth, pour into the wok and stir. This will help thicken the sauce. Serve.

Discard any uneaten rice immediately. Store the sweet and sour chicken in the refrigerator for up to 2 days, or freeze extra portions in small sealable containers, label and use within 1 month. To use from frozen, carefully defrost. Heat through fully before serving.

Makes 6–8 child portions or 2 adult portions

shepherd's pie

see variations page 262

This favourite British or Irish dish is traditionally made with minced lamb topped with a crust of mashed potato. The term 'shepherd's pie' refers to the meat used being lamb.

1 tbsp sunflower oil
1 onion, peeled and finely chopped
1 carrot, peeled and finely chopped
175 g (6 oz) lean minced lamb
1 tsp chopped fresh thyme
pinch ground cinnamon

225 ml (8 fl. oz) low-sodium lamb or beef stock
1 tsp tomato paste
4 tbsp frozen peas
450 g (1 lb) potatoes, peeled and chopped
2 tbsp butter
4 tbsp grated Cheddar cheese

Heat the oil in a nonstick frying pan over medium heat. Sauté the onion and carrot for 5 minutes, until softened. Transfer to a large saucepan with lid. Break up the lamb and add to the pan. Cook for 4–5 minutes, stirring often to break the meat into tiny pieces. Transfer to the saucepan, and place over medium heat. Add the thyme, cinnamon, stock, tomato paste and frozen peas. Bring to the boil. Reduce to a simmer, cover and cook for 30–40 minutes. Cook the potatoes in boiling water for 20 minutes, until soft. Drain, return to the pan, add the butter and mash. Preheat the oven to 200°C (400°F/Gas mark 6). Transfer the meat mixture to a baking dish. Spread the mashed potatoes evenly over the meat. With a fork, fluff up the potatoes. Sprinkle with cheese and bake for 20–25 minutes, until the cheese has melted and the potato crust is golden brown. Serve.

Store in the refrigerator for up to 2 days, or freeze extra portions in small sealable containers, label, and use within 1 month. Carefully defrost and heat through fully before serving.

Makes 6–8 child portions or 2–3 adult portions

lasagne

see variations page 263

This dish is always a popular family meal. Serve it with a crisp green salad for the adults.

1 tbsp sunflower oil
1 onion, peeled and finely chopped
1 carrot, peeled and finely chopped
1 red pepper, deseeded and finely chopped
100 g (4 oz) mushrooms, finely chopped
450 g (1 lb) lean minced beef

1 (400-g/14-oz) tin chopped tomatoes
1 tbsp tomato paste
225 ml (8 fl. oz) low-sodium beef stock
6–8 fresh lasagne sheets (or use dried)
1 quantity cheese sauce (page 191)
50 g (2 oz) finely grated Parmesan cheese

Heat the oil in a nonstick frying pan over medium heat. Add the onion and carrot and sauté for 5 minutes, until softened and starting to brown. Transfer to a large saucepan. Add the pepper and mushrooms to the pan, and sauté for 2–3 minutes. Transfer to the saucepan.

Break up the beef and add to the pan. Cook for 4–5 minutes, stirring. Transfer to the saucepan, and place over medium heat and add the chopped tomatoes, paste and stock. Stir and bring to the boil. Reduce to a simmer, cover and cook for 30–40 minutes. Purée.

Preheat the oven to 200°C (400°F/Gas mark 6). Cover the bottom of a baking dish with part of the meat sauce, then cover with lasagne sheets. Continue to layer the meat sauce and pasta, finishing with pasta. Pour the cheese sauce over the pasta, sprinkle with cheese and bake in the oven for 15–20 minutes until the top is golden brown and the cheese is bubbling.

Makes 8–10 child portions or 3–4 adult portions

beef meatballs

see variations page 264

For younger babies these can be mashed. Once the baby moves on to finger food, these are lovely to hold and nibble. They can be served on their own or with the Classic Tomato Sauce (page 69) or Mediterranean Roasted Vegetables (page 70).

900 g (2 lb) lean minced beef
pinch freshly ground black pepper
3 tbsp sunflower oil

Preheat the oven to 175°C (350°F/Gas mark 4). Mix the lean minced beef with a pinch of black pepper. Roll the mixture into 2.5-cm (1-in) balls.

Heat the oil in a nonstick frying pan over medium heat. Carefully fry the meatballs, gently rolling them around the pan, to just sear and lightly colour them. Do not allow them to brown, or they will be hard for babies with no teeth to chew.

Transfer to a deep baking dish, cover with kitchen foil, and bake for 10–15 minutes until thoroughly cooked. The foil will prevent the meatballs from browning. Remove from the oven and serve warm.

The meatballs can be refrigerated for up to 2 days or freeze extra portions in freezer-proof containers, label and use within 1 month. To use from frozen, carefully defrost. Heat through fully before serving.

Makes 30–40 meatballs

pizza

see variations page 265

Nothing beats homemade pizza. Using the same bread dough base as you used for breadsticks (page 130), you can make pizza or calzones for the whole family. Let your children, even toddlers, help you. Give them their own ball of dough to knead and roll out, and let them choose their toppings to make their own personal pizza.

for the pizza dough
1 quantity breadstick dough (page 130)

for the topping
¹⁄₃ quantity of Classic Tomato Sauce (page 69)
fresh basil leaves
240 g (8¹⁄₂ oz) grated mozzarella cheese

Make the pizza dough. After it has doubled in size, knock back (press out any air bubbles) and divide into 3 or 4 balls.

Preheat oven to 220°C (425°F/Gas mark 7). With a rolling pin, roll out each ball to a circle shape and top with tomato sauce, fresh basil leaves and mozzarella cheese. Bake on a nonstick baking tray for 15–20 minutes, until the cheese has melted.

Make and freeze extra pizzas in freezer-proof containers, label and use within 1 month. To use from frozen, carefully defrost. Heat through fully before serving.

Makes 3–4 small pizzas

mini quiches

see variations page 266

Quiche is delicious for the whole family. This recipe makes 12 mini quiches.

for the pastry
225 g (8 oz) plain flour, plus extra for
    rolling out
4 tbsp white vegetable fat
50 g (2 oz) butter
1 tbsp cold water

for the filling
100 ml (4 fl. oz) milk
1 egg
50 g (2 oz) grated Cheddar cheese

Preheat the oven to 175°C (350°F/Gas mark 4). Grease a 12-cup mini muffin tin. Rub the vegetable fat and butter into the flour, using your fingers, until the mixture resembles breadcrumbs. Add half the water and mix to make a dough. Add water slowly until the dough comes together. Dust a clean work surface with a little flour and tip the dough onto it. Sprinkle the dough and your hands with a little flour. With a rolling pin, roll out the dough until it is about 5 mm (¼ in) thick. Cut out 12 circles of pastry and press the circles into the cups. Place baking beans on the pastry and bake for 10 minutes, until golden brown. Remove from the oven.

Beat the milk and eggs together, add the grated cheese. Pour into the baked crusts. Bake for 15–20 minutes. The pastry should be golden brown and the egg mixture set. Remove from the oven and allow to cool slightly before serving. Store in the refrigerator for up to 3 days, or freeze for up to 1 month. Carefully defrost and heat through fully before serving.

Makes 12 mini quiches

focaccia

see variations page 267

This Italian flatbread is easy for little hands to hold, lovely dunked in homemade tomato sauce (see page 69), and great as a base for garlic bread. It's best eaten the same day it is made.

dough for breadsticks (page 130)
olive oil for drizzling

Prepare the dough for breadsticks and let it rise until doubled. Preheat the oven to 220°C (425°F/Gas mark 7).

Knock the dough back (make sure there are no air bubbles) and split into four equal parts. With a rolling pin, roll out each part into an oval, approximately 1-cm (½-in) thick. With your finger, press indentations in the top, then drizzle the top with olive oil.

Place each oval on a greased baking pan and bake for 15–20 minutes until golden brown. Remove and allow to cool.

Once cooled, store the focaccia in an airtight container for up to 3 days, but note that they are best eaten the same day. Alternatively, as soon as they have cooled, freeze for up to 1 month. To use from frozen, carefully defrost. Heat through fully before serving.

Makes 4 focaccia

cheese biscuits

see variations page 268

This recipe is excellent for making with younger children. Cheese biscuits are lovely eaten warm from the oven, split in half and spread with butter, or eaten cold on a picnic or as part of a packed lunch.

150 g (5 oz) self-raising flour
25 g (1 oz) butter
50 g (2 oz) grated Cheddar cheese

2 tbsp milk
1 egg

Preheat the oven to 175°C (350°F/Gas mark 4). With your fingers, rub in the butter into the flour until the mixture resembles breadcrumbs. Stir in the grated cheese. Stir in the milk and egg until the mixture forms a dough.

Dust a clean work surface with a little flour and tip the dough onto it. Sprinkle the dough and your hands with a little flour too. Gently flatten the dough with your hands or a rolling pin until it is approximately 4 cm (1½ in) thick. Use a 7.5-cm (3-in) round biscuit cutter to cut out the biscuits, or cut into 8 wedges with a knife. Reroll and recut any extra dough.

Grease a baking tray and transfer the biscuits onto it. Bake for 12–15 minutes, until they are golden brown and well risen. Once cooled, store the biscuits in an airtight container, but note that they are best eaten the same day. Alternatively, as soon as they have cooled, freeze for up to 1 month. To use from frozen, carefully defrost. Heat through fully before serving.

Makes 4 cheese biscuits

savoury cheese muffins

see variations page 269

These make a refreshing change from sandwiches, and are a great recipe for toddlers and children to help you make. Just stirring the mixture will help them feel as if they are doing real cooking, and they will be much more willing to try eating the muffins.

225 g (8 oz) self-raising flour
1 tsp baking powder
100 g (4 oz) grated cheese such as Cheddar

1 egg
175 ml (6 fl. oz) milk
60 g (2½ oz) butter, melted

Preheat the oven to 175°C (350°F/Gas mark 4). Prepare a regular-size muffin tin or a mini-muffin pan with paper baking cups or by greasing the pan.

Mix together the flour, baking powder and grated cheese. Beat the egg, add the milk and melted butter and beat well. Pour mixture into the dry ingredients. Mix well, but don't worry if there are any lumps, as they will even out during cooking. Evenly fill the muffin cups. Bake regular size muffins for 15–20 minutes until golden and firm to the touch (10–15 minutes for mini muffins). When a toothpick inserted in the centre of a muffin comes out clean, remove the pan from the oven. Allow muffins to cool before removing from pan.

Once cooled, store the muffins in an airtight container, but note that they are best eaten the same day. Alternatively, as soon as they have cooled, freeze for up to 1 month. To use from frozen, carefully defrost. Heat through fully before serving.

Makes 12 regular or 24 mini muffins

soda bread

see variations page 270

This quick and easy bread uses baking soda and cream of tartar as a rising agent. It's great to use for an emergency alternative to bread and also a good recipe to encourage toddlers to help in the kitchen.

425 g (15 oz) plain flour, plus a little extra	½ tsp sugar
1 tsp bicarbonate of soda	25 g (1 oz) butter, melted
2 tsp cream of tartar	275 ml (10 fl. oz) milk

Preheat the oven to 190°C (375°F/Gas mark 5). Grease a baking tray. In a large bowl, mix together the flour, bicarbonate of soda, cream of tartar and sugar. Make a well in the centre of the dry ingredients and add the melted butter and milk. Use your hands to mix everything together to form a soft dough.

Dust a clean work surface with a little flour and tip the dough onto it. Sprinkle the dough and your hands with a little flour. Divide the dough into 8 lumps for large soda bread or 12 for smaller ones. Leave the lumps rough, as this is how soda bread is meant to look; it's not meant to be rounded. Place the lumps of dough onto the prepared baking tray, leaving space around them to expand. Bake for 20–30 minutes until the bread is golden brown.

The bread does not keep very well and is best eaten warm from the oven. It freezes well if frozen on the day it is made, and used within 1 month. To use from frozen, carefully defrost. Heat through fully before serving.

Makes 8 regular or 12 small soda breads

cheddar palmiers

see variations page 271

These cheese pastries are easy to make using ready-made puff pastry. Palmier is French for palm tree, and these pastries are in the shape of a palm leaf or butterfly. They are the same no matter what they are called, and guaranteed to please little ones.

1 sheet prepared puff pastry
25 g (1 oz) finely grated Parmesan cheese

Preheat the oven to 220°C (425°F/Gas mark 7). Grease 1 or 2 baking trays. With a rolling pin, roll out the pastry to form an oblong approximately 10 x 15 cm (4 x 6 in). Sprinkle $^2/_3$ of the cheese over the pastry, and gently press the cheese into the pastry. Fold over each end to meet in the centre of the pastry. Sprinkle the rest of the cheese onto the pastry, then fold (roll) up again. Do not press down on the pastry. This should give you two rolls of pastry that meet in the centre.

Use a sharp knife to cut across the rolls into 3-mm ($^1/_8$-in) wide strips. Lay them on their side on the prepared baking tray, leaving space around them to spread. Bake for 8–10 minutes, until golden brown. Transfer to a cooling rack and leave until completely cooled.

Store in an airtight container. They will keep for up to 1 week. If you prefer, the palmiers can be frozen before baking. After cutting them, stack with pieces of parchment or waxed paper between to prevent them from sticking. Freeze for up to 1 month, defrost thoroughly before cooking.

Makes 10–12 palmiers

griddle scones

see variations page 272

These are also known as drop scones (you 'drop' spoonfuls of batter onto a hot pan), girdle scones in Scotland (named after the 'girdle' they are traditionally cooked on), or blinis. These are a sweet version. They can be given to babies less than 12 months old if you use breast milk or formula instead of cow's milk, and serve plain.

225 g (8 oz) self-raising flour
2 eggs

5–6 tbsp milk (use breast milk or formula for babies under 12 months)
butter for frying

Put the flour in a large bowl. Make a well in the centre of the flour, add the eggs and begin beating with a whisk, gradually taking more flour from around the edges of the well. Add the milk, one tablespoon at a time, whisking it into the flour until you have a soft dropping consistency.

Heat a teaspoon of butter in a frying pan set on medium–high heat. Drop tablespoonfuls of the mixture into the pan. You should be able to cook 6 or 7 scones at the same time. Cook for 3–4 minutes. When bubbles form on the surface, turn the scone over. The scone will immediately rise up a little. Cook for another 2–3 minutes, until both sides are golden brown. Remove from the pan. Serve with butter, jam, syrup, lemon juice or just on their own.

Store for up to 3 days in an airtight container or they can be frozen for 1 month. To use from frozen, carefully defrost. Heat through fully before serving.

Makes 12 griddle scones

oaty biscuits

see variations page 273

These biscuits are a great way to encourage your toddler to help you cook. Make sure that the mixture has cooled before letting your toddler roll the mixture into balls and flatten them onto the baking sheet. With the addition of the oats and raisins, these biscuits are slightly healthier than typical biscuits.

85 g (3½ oz) butter
50 g (2 oz) light brown sugar
50 g (2 oz) maple syrup
100 g (4 oz) self-raising flour

225 g (8 oz) quick-cooking porridge oats
½ tsp ground cinnamon
½ tsp ground nutmeg
50 g (2 oz) golden raisins, chopped

Preheat the oven to 200°C (400°F/Gas mark 6). Grease a baking tray. Melt the butter, sugar and syrup in a small saucepan over medium heat. In a bowl, combine the flour, oats, spices and raisins. Pour in the melted mixture, and mix to a dough.

Place teaspoonfuls of the dough onto the prepared tray. You should have enough for 12–16 biscuits. Gently flatten the tops. Bake for 10–15 minutes until golden brown. Remove from the oven and allow to cool completely.

Keep in an airtight container for 3–4 days or freeze the day they are made for up to 1 month. To use from frozen, carefully defrost, allow to come to room temperature and serve.

Makes 12–16 biscuits

fruit muffins

see variations page 274

These muffins contain fresh fruit, making them slightly healthier than plain muffins; however, they are still high in sugar and fat and should be eaten in moderation.

150 g (5 oz) fresh or thawed frozen berries
    (blueberries for babies up to 12 months;
    raspberries, strawberries, and blackcurrants
    for toddlers)
225 g (8 oz) self-raising flour

1 tsp baking powder
150 g (5 oz) light brown sugar
1 egg
175 ml (6 fl. oz) milk
60 g (2½ oz) butter, melted

Preheat the oven to 175°C (350°F/Gas mark 4). Prepare a regular-size muffin tin or a mini-muffin pan with paper baking cups or by greasing the pan. Wash the berries and remove stems if necessary.

In a bowl, mix together the flour, baking powder and brown sugar. Add the berries and stir gently to mix. In a separate bowl, beat the egg, add the milk and beat well. Add the melted butter and stir to combine. Pour mixture into the dry ingredients. Mix well; don't worry if there are any lumps, as they will even out during cooking. Evenly fill the muffin cups. Bake regular-size muffins for 15–20 minutes until golden and firm to the touch (10–15 minutes for mini muffins). When a toothpick inserted in the centre of a muffin comes out clean, remove the tin from the oven. Allow muffins to cool before removing from pan.

Store in an airtight container for up to 3 days or freeze immediately and use within 1 month. To use from frozen, carefully defrost. Heat through before serving if wished.

Makes 12 regular or 24 mini muffins

gingerbread men

see variations page 275

Gingerbread men are traditionally made during winter, using warming spices such as ginger, cinnamon, cloves and nutmeg. This is a good recipe to make with children.

185 g (6½ oz) plain flour
1 tsp ground ginger
½ tsp bicarbonate of soda
50 g (2 oz) butter
100 g (4 oz) sugar

1 egg yolk
2 tbsp black treacle
2 tbsp icing sugar
juice of ½ lemon
raisins or small sweets for decoration

Preheat the oven to 175°C (350°F/Gas mark 4). Mix together the flour, ginger and bicarbonate of soda. Rub in the butter until the mixture resembles breadcrumbs. Stir in the sugar. Mix the egg yolk and treacle together and add to the mixture. Stir to mix, and then use your hands to work into a ball of dough. Sprinkle a little flour onto a clean work surface and knead the dough until it is smooth. With a rolling pin, roll out the dough until it is 5 mm (¼ in) thick. Use a gingerbread man cutter to cut out shapes.

Transfer the gingerbread men to a greased, lined baking tray. Bake for 10–12 minutes until golden brown. Remove from the oven and leave the gingerbread men for 5–10 minutes to allow them to harden before moving to a cooling rack. Once the biscuits have cooled, mix icing using icing sugar and freshly squeezed lemon juice. Pipe onto the gingerbread men to make faces and clothes. Use raisins or small sweets for buttons.

Place uncooked dough in a freezer bag and freeze for up to 1 month. Cooked gingerbread men can be stored in an airtight container for up to 1 week, or frozen for up to 1 month. To use from frozen, carefully defrost. Heat through before serving.

Makes 12 gingerbread men

thumbprint cookies

see variations page 276

These biscuits are a good recipe for older toddlers to help with. They can rub in the fat and flour and stir in the egg, and they can even form the shapes of the biscuits. You could use a food processor if you want, but that's no fun for a toddler.

225 g (8 oz) self-raising flour	1 egg
100 g (4 oz) cold butter	2 tbsp milk
75 g (3 oz) sugar	raspberry jam

Preheat the oven to 200°C (400°F/Gas mark 6). Grease a baking tray. Place the flour and butter in a bowl and rub the flour and butter through your fingers (adding a bit more flour if necessary), until the mixture resembles breadcrumbs. Stir in the sugar. Beat the egg and add it to the mixture. Add a little milk at a time, stirring or working with your hands, until you have a soft dough. If the dough is too dry, add a little extra milk.

Place teaspoonfuls of the mixture onto the prepared tray. You should have enough for 12 biscuits. The biscuits will double in size, so leave space between them. Gently flatten the top and make an indentation with a clean finger in the centre. Place a little raspberry jam into the indentation. Bake for 15–20 minutes until golden brown.

Remove and allow to cool. Keep in an airtight container for 3–4 days or freeze the day they are made, for up to 1 month. Carefully defrost, allow to come to room temperature and serve.

Makes 12 biscuits

pineapple kebabs with yoghurt

see variations page 277

These fruity kebabs are gently cooked to release their juices and flavours. They are a great way to tempt children to try different fruit. Remove the skewers before giving the fruit to toddlers and young children, as they are dangerous.

½ pineapple
50 g (2 oz) dark brown sugar
pinch ground cinnamon

juice of 1 lemon or lime
1 tbsp thick Greek yoghurt
1 tsp honey

Soak 4 bamboo skewers in water for at least 30 minutes. Peel, core and cut the pineapple into 2.5-cm (1-in) chunks.

Mix together the brown sugar, cinnamon and lemon or lime juice in a saucepan. Cook over low heat, until the sugar dissolves.

Thread the pineapple chunks onto the skewers and brush all over with the sugar mixture. Bake in the oven or cook on a barbecue grill for 3–4 minutes on each side, until the fruit starts to brown. Cut the pineapple pieces smaller if serving to young toddlers.

Mix together the yoghurt and honey to serve as a dip with the kebabs.

Store in the refrigerator for up to 3 days.

Makes 4 portions

peach cobbler

see variations page 278

A cobbler is a deep-dish fruit dessert with a biscuit crust. The topping is deliberately left lumpy to achieve the 'cobbled' effect that gives the dessert its name. Older toddlers love to help mix the dough. It is lovely served with plain yoghurt.

4 ripe peaches, peeled, pitted and chopped
juice of 1 lemon
1 tbsp granulated sugar
pinch ground cinnamon
1 tbsp water

for the topping
150 g (5 oz) flour
100 g (4 oz) cold butter
½ tsp baking powder
50 g (2 oz) granulated sugar
100 ml (4 fl. oz) buttermilk
a little brown sugar for sprinkling

Preheat the oven to 175°C (350°F/Gas mark 4). Place the peaches in a saucepan with the lemon juice, sugar, cinnamon and water. Set the pan over low heat and cook for 5 minutes until the peaches are soft. Transfer to a 1.7-litre (3-pint) baking dish.

To make the topping, place the flour and butter into a bowl. Rub the butter and flour together, using your fingertips, until the mixture resembles breadcrumbs. Stir in the baking powder and sugar. Add the buttermilk. The mixture will be lumpy. Place spoonfuls of the cobbler topping on the peaches. Sprinkle with brown sugar and bake for 20–25 minutes, until golden brown. Serve warm.

Store in the refrigerator for up to 3 days or freeze for up to 1 month. To use from frozen, carefully defrost, heat through fully before serving.

Makes 4–5 child portions or 2 adult portions

chocolate ice cream

see variations page 279

Homemade ice cream tastes much better than the commercial kind. You do not need an ice cream maker. All you need is a freezer and a lazy day at home to keep churning.

4 egg yolks
100 g (4 oz) sugar
225 ml (8 fl. oz) milk

150 g (5 oz) plain chocolate chips
225 ml (8 fl. oz) heavy cream

Whisk the egg yolks and sugar until they are thick and leave a trail when you remove the whisk. Pour the milk into a saucepan, set over medium heat and bring to the boil. As soon as it boils, remove it from the heat. Pour the egg yolk mixture into the hot milk, whisking constantly. Set the saucepan on low heat and stir continuously until the mixture coats the back of the spoon. Do not let it boil or the mixture will curdle. Remove the pan from the hob, and allow to cool. In a separate pan, heat the chocolate chips over a low heat until liquid; do not allow to bubble. Add the chocolate and the cream to the egg yolk and milk mixture, stirring well. Put it into the refrigerator to chill for around 2 hours until cold.

To freeze with an ice cream maker: tollow the manufacturer's instructions, then transfer to a freezer container and set in the freezer for 30 minutes to firm up before serving.

To freeze without an ice cream maker: Pour the mixture into a suitable freezer container and place in the freezer. After 1 hour, remove the container, pour the contents into a bowl, and whisk to break down the ice crystals. This step is necessary so that you end up with smooth ice cream. Pour the mixture back into the freezer container and freeze. Repeat every hour for the next 4 hours, then the ice cream will be ready to serve. Consume within 1 month.
Makes 1 quart

compôte

see variations page 280

A compôte is usually made by slowly cooking fresh or dried fruit in a sugar syrup, which may include spices. In this recipe, I have omitted the sugar syrup and substituted apple juice (for babies under 12 months) or orange juice. It can be served warm or chilled, for breakfast with muesli and yoghurt or for dessert with yoghurt, whipped cream or ice cream. It is a great way to encourage toddlers to eat fruit.

400 g (14 oz) dried fruit (such as raisins, apples, prunes, figs, cranberries, cherries, apricots)

1 cinnamon stick
3 whole cloves
450 ml (16 fl. oz) orange or apple juice

Place all the ingredients in a small saucepan, set it over medium heat, cover and cook gently for 15–20 minutes, stirring occasionally, until the fruit is plump. Add a little more juice if the mixture looks like it is drying out.

Remove the cinnamon stick and the cloves. Purée the mixture for young babies. Serve warm or chilled.

Store in the refrigerator for up to 3 days or freeze for up to 1 month. To use from frozen, carefully defrost. Heat through fully before serving.

Makes 4 child portions or 2 adult portions

rhubarb fool

see variations page 281

A fool is traditionally made with cooked, puréed fruit mixed with whipped cream and chilled. This version uses yoghurt and crème fraîche, making it a little healthier. Rhubarb is the only vegetable we eat as a fruit. (We eat the stalk of the plant, so it is a vegetable, as fruits contain the seeds of the plant.) Rhubarb can be a little slimy for young palates, so mixing it with the yoghurt makes it easier to eat. Hint: for older toddlers, try dunking raw fresh young rhubarb in brown sugar. It has a tangy citrus flavour.

200 g (7 oz) fresh rhubarb chopped into
   2.5-cm (1-in) pieces
1 tbsp light brown sugar
1 tbsp water

100 ml (4 fl. oz) crème fraîche
100 ml (4 fl. oz) natural yoghurt
1 tbsp icing sugar

Place the rhubarb in a saucepan along with the brown sugar and water, and simmer for 5–10 minutes, until tender and collapsed. Purée in a blender or food processor.

Whip the crème fraîche and yoghurt together until it forms soft peaks, then gently stir in the icing sugar. Gently stir in the rhubarb purée, transfer to 4 small bowls, chill and serve.

Store in the refrigerator for up to 3 days, or place extra portions in freezer-proof containers and freeze for up to 1 month. To defrost, simply remove from the freezer and allow to come to room temperature, stir and serve.

Makes 4 child portions

variations

breakfast muffins

see base recipe page 161

breakfast muffins with dates & apple
Prepare the basic recipe, replacing the carrots with 8 very finely chopped dates.
Reduce the sugar to 75 g (3 oz).

breakfast muffins with carrots & raisins
Prepare the basic recipe, replacing the apples with 50 g (2 oz) raisins.

breakfast muffins with sweet potato, orange & raisins
Peel, chop and steam 2 sweet potatoes for 20 minutes until soft, then mash
with a fork. Prepare the basic recipe, adding the grated zest of 1 orange and
50 g (2 oz) raisins. Mix the juice from the orange with 100 g (4 oz) icing sugar
to make a thin icing to drizzle over each cooled muffin.

breakfast muffins with orange & honey
Prepare the basic recipe, replacing the carrots and apple with the zest and juice
of 2 oranges, and the brown sugar with 3 tablespoons honey.

variations

bircher muesli

see base recipe page 163

bircher muesli with banana
Prepare the basic recipe. Peel and mash 1 banana, and stir it through the muesli just before serving (or puréeing for baby).

bircher muesli with mango
Prepare the basic recipe. Peel and mash 1 ripe mango, and stir it through the muesli just before serving (or puréeing for baby).

bircher muesli with dried fruit
Prepare the basic recipe. Cook 2 dried apricots and 1 tablespoon raisins in a little water for 4–5 minutes, until plump. Purée and add to the muesli.

bircher muesli with pear
Prepare the basic recipe, replacing the apple with 1 washed, peeled, cored and grated ripe pear.

bircher muesli with berries
Prepare the basic recipe. Squash or mash 1 tablespoon blueberries, and stir them through the muesli just before serving (or puréeing for baby).

variations

granola bars

see base recipe page 164

granola bars with shredded apple
Prepare the basic recipe, adding 1 peeled and finely grated apple to the mixture
along with ½ teaspoon ground cinnamon.

granola bars with raisins
Prepare the basic recipe, using half golden raisins and half dark raisins.

granola bars with dried apricots
Prepare the basic recipe, using half golden raisins and half finely chopped
dried apricots.

granola bars with dried cranberries & hazelnuts
Prepare the basic recipe, replacing the raisins with dried cranberries and the
pecans with chopped hazelnuts.

variations

cream cheese pinwheels

see base recipe page 166

cream cheese & jam pinwheels
Prepare the basic recipe, spreading a thin layer of jam over the cream cheese before rolling up.

cheesy tomato pinwheels
Prepare the basic recipe, spreading ½ teaspoon tomato paste on the cream cheese before rolling up.

guacamole pinwheels
Prepare the basic recipe, replacing the cream cheese with a thin layer of guacamole (page 171).

egg salad pinwheels
Instead of the basic recipe, omit the cream cheese. Hard-boil 1 egg, then mash half the egg with 1 teaspoon mayonnaise. Spread the egg salad thinly on the bread before rolling up.

hummus pinwheels
Prepare the basic recipe, replacing the cream cheese with a thin layer of hummus (page 173).

butter bean dip with tortilla chips

see base recipe page 168

butter bean dip with salmon
Prepare the basic recipe, adding 1 cooked salmon fillet to the blender or food processor.

butter bean dip with chicken
Prepare the basic recipe, adding 1 cooked, chopped chicken breast and 1 additional tablespoon natural yoghurt to the blender or food processor.

butter bean dip with lemon & tahini
Prepare the basic recipe, adding the zest and juice of 1 lemon and 1 teaspoon tahini paste to the mixture in the blender or food processor. (Do not use this variation for anyone with sesame seed allergy.)

butter bean dip with lemon & coriander
Prepare the basic recipe, adding the zest and juice of 1 lemon and replacing the parsley with coriander.

butter bean dip with sun-dried tomato
Prepare the basic recipe, adding 4 chopped, drained sun-dried tomatoes to the blender or food processor.

variations

tahini dip

see base recipe page 170

lemon tahini dip
Prepare the basic recipe, replacing half the water with the juice of 1 lemon.

tahini & hummus
Prepare the basic recipe, adding 1 tablespoon of your favourite hummus (page 173) to make a tasty thin dipping sauce. This is great for those who prefer thinner dips to hummus.

tahini & paprika dip
Prepare the basic recipe, adding ½ teaspoon mild paprika to the dip.

tahini with cumin & coriander dip
Prepare the basic recipe, adding ¼ teaspoon each of ground cumin and ground coriander.

variations

baby guacamole

see base recipe page 171

lime guacamole
Prepare the basic recipe, replacing the lemon with the juice of 1 lime.

lime & chilli guacamole
Prepare the basic recipe, replacing the lemon with the juice of 1 lime and adding a pinch of chilli powder.

tomato guacamole
Prepare the basic recipe, adding 1 skinned and finely chopped tomato to the guacamole.

roasted red pepper guacamole
Prepare the basic recipe, adding 1 roasted and puréed red pepper. To roast the pepper, wash and halve it and remove seeds. Cut each half into 3 slices. Bake at 220°C (425°F/Gas mark 7) for 30–35 minutes, until the peppers are slightly browned at the edges. Transfer the peppers to a plastic freezer-proof bag, tie the top closed, and leave for 5 minutes. Then remove the skin and purée.

hummus

see base recipe page 173

beetroot hummus
Prepare the basic recipe, adding 1 washed, peeled, and grated raw beetroot to the blender or food processor.

roasted onion hummus
Prepare the basic recipe, adding roasted onion to the blender or food processor. To prepare the onion, peel and cut 1 onion into sixths, drizzle with a little olive oil and roast on a baking tray at 200°C (400°F/Gas mark 6) for 20–25 minutes, until soft and slightly brown at the edges.

lemon & coriander hummus
Prepare the basic recipe, adding the juice of 1 lemon and 1 tablespoon chopped fresh coriander to the blender or food processor.

roasted red pepper hummus
Prepare the basic recipe, adding 1 roasted and puréed red pepper (see directions page 245, guacamole variation).

sun-dried tomato hummus
Prepare the basic recipe, adding 3–4 chopped, drained sun-dried tomatoes to the blender or food processor.

mackerel pâté

see base recipe page 174

mackerel & tomato pâté
Prepare the basic recipe, adding 1 teaspoon tomato paste.

sardine pâté
Prepare the basic recipe, replacing the mackerel with 1 small tin of sardines in tomato sauce. Make sure you first remove the bones.

tuna pâté
Prepare the basic recipe, replacing the mackerel with 1 small tin of tuna in water, drained.

salmon pâté
Prepare the basic recipe, replacing the mackerel with 1 cooked salmon fillet or a small tin of salmon, drained.

variations

oatcakes

see base recipe page 177

parmesan oatcakes
Prepare the basic recipe, adding 1 tablespoon finely grated Parmesan cheese.

rosemary oatcakes
Prepare the basic recipe, adding 1 teaspoon chopped dried rosemary.

sesame seed oatcakes
Prepare the basic recipe, adding 1 tablespoon sesame seeds (not for anyone with a sesame seed allergy, or for under 12 months).

pumpkin seed oatcakes
Prepare the basic recipe, adding 1 tablespoon pumpkin seeds.

sunflower seed oatcakes
Prepare the basic recipe, adding 1 tablespoon sunflower seeds.

roasted red pepper & tomato soup

see base recipe page 179

roasted red pepper, tomato & courgette soup
Prepare the basic recipe, adding slices of ½ courgette to the baking tray with the other vegetables.

roasted red pepper & tomato soup with basil
Prepare the basic recipe, adding 1 tablespoon chopped fresh basil to the stock.

roasted red pepper & tomato soup with rice
Prepare the basic recipe. Serve it with rice to make a substantial meal. My son liked this when he was little and named it 'ice and soup' because he couldn't pronounce his Rs very well.

roasted red pepper & tomato soup with macaroni
Prepare the basic recipe. Stir in some cooked macaroni or other small pasta shapes.

roasted red pepper & tomato soup with sausage balls
Prepare the basic recipe. Roll a little good-quality sausage meat into balls. Put on a baking tray and roast in the oven for 15–20 minutes until thoroughly cooked. Serve with the soup.

variations

mini-minestrone

see base recipe page 180

minestrone with rice
Prepare the basic recipe, replacing the pasta with 100 g (4 oz) rice.

minestrone with cheese croutons
Prepare the basic recipe. Cut a few thin slices of Cheddar or another hard cheese. Toast bread under the grill, turn over, lay the cheese on the untoasted side and toast until the cheese melts and begins to bubble. Cut into fingers or cubes and float on top of each soup serving.

minestrone with meatballs
Prepare the basic recipe. While the soup is cooking, roll 150 g (5 oz) lean minced beef, lamb or pork into walnut-sized balls. Fry the meatballs in a nonstick frying pan for 5–6 minutes, until cooked through. Add the meatballs to the soup just before serving.

minestrone with cabbage
Prepare the basic recipe, replacing the courgette with ¼ head chopped Savoy cabbage.

minestrone with peas & leeks
Prepare the basic recipe, replacing the courgette with 1 tablespoon fresh or frozen peas and ½ chopped leek (white part).

variations

fish chowder

see base recipe page 183

fish & corn chowder
Prepare the basic recipe, adding 100 g (4 oz) corn kernels (fresh, frozen or tinned) when you add the fish.

salmon chowder
Prepare the basic recipe, replacing the white fish fillet with a salmon fillet. (Do not give babies salmon until they have had white fish.)

fish & leek chowder
Prepare the basic recipe, replacing the onion with ½ leek.

chicken & corn chowder
Prepare the basic recipe, replacing the fish fillet with 1 chopped chicken breast. Add the chicken to the soup at the same time as the potatoes. Add 100 g (4 oz) corn kernels (fresh, frozen, or tinned) 5 minutes before the end of the cooking time.

chicken & sweet potato chowder
Prepare the basic recipe, replacing the fish fillet with 1 chopped chicken breast, added to the soup at the same time as the potatoes. Replace the potato with 1 small sweet potato.

variations

pasta with pea pesto

see base recipe page 184

pasta with creamy mushroom pasta sauce
Instead of the basic recipe, sauté 225 g (8 oz) chopped mushrooms and ½ onion, sliced, in 1 tablespoon olive oil over medium heat for 5–10 minutes until soft. Purée and mix with 75 g (3 oz) crème fraîche.

pasta with basil pesto
Instead of the basic recipe, put 75 g (3 oz) fresh basil leaves, 1 tablespoon pine nuts, and 50 g (2 oz) finely grated Parmesan cheese in a food processor. Process to a paste and stir in the crème fraîche.

pasta with red pepper pesto
Instead of the basic recipe, roast 1 sweet red pepper (see directions page 245, guacamole variation). Purée the pulp with 1 tablespoon pine nuts and 50 g (2 oz) finely grated Parmesan cheese. Stir in the crème fraîche.

pasta with sun-dried tomato pesto
Instead of the basic recipe, purée 6 sun-dried tomato halves with 1 tablespoon pine nuts and 50 g (2 oz) finely grated Parmesan. Stir in the crème fraîche.

variations

aubergine bake

see base recipe page 186

aubergine bake with mushrooms
Prepare the basic recipe, adding 4 tablespoons sliced mushrooms in a layer
on top of the aubergine.

aubergine bake with chicken
Prepare the basic recipe, adding 1 cooked, sliced chicken breast in a layer
on top of the aubergine.

aubergine bake with chicken and mozzarella
Prepare the basic recipe, adding 1 cooked, sliced chicken breast in a layer
on top of the aubergine, and replacing the Parmesan with an additional
4 tablespoons mozzarella.

aubergine bake with lentils
Prepare the basic recipe, adding 175 g (6 oz) cooked puy or green lentils
in a layer on top of the aubergine.

variations

veggie korma

see base recipe page 188

vegetable korma with beans
Prepare the basic recipe, replacing the potato with 100 g (4 oz) mixed cooked beans, such as kidney or cannellini.

vegetable korma with sweet potato
Prepare the basic recipe, replacing the potato with 1 small sweet potato.

vegetable korma with chicken
Prepare the basic recipe, replacing the potato with 1 chopped skinless and boneless chicken breast.

vegetable korma with cauliflower
Prepare the basic recipe, replacing the potato with 100 g (4 oz) cauliflower florets. Reduce the vegetable cooking time to 10 minutes.

vegetable korma with courgette
Prepare the basic recipe, replacing the carrot with 1 courgette, finely chopped.

vegetable korma with baby spinach
Prepare the basic recipe, adding 100 g (4 oz) of baby spinach leaves, washed and chopped, when you stir in the cream and coriander.

variations

macaroni cheese

see base recipe page 191

macaroni cheese with roasted peppers
Prepare the basic recipe, adding 1 roasted red pepper (see directions page 245, guacamole variation), finely chopped or puréed, to the baking dish.

macaroni cheese with sun-dried tomatoes
Prepare the basic recipe, adding 4 drained and finely chopped sun-dried tomatoes to the baking dish.

macaroni cheese with chicken
Prepare the basic recipe, adding 1 cooked and chopped chicken breast to the baking dish.

macaroni cheese with grape tomatoes
Prepare the basic recipe, adding 100 g (4 oz) finely chopped grape tomatoes to the baking dish.

macaroni cheese with roasted aubergine
Prepare the basic recipe, adding 1 chopped and roasted small aubergine to the baking dish. To roast aubergine, wash and chop it, then place on a baking pan, drizzle with olive oil and cook in a hot oven (220°C/425°F/Gas mark 7) for 15–20 minutes, until soft.

variations

homemade baked beans

see base recipe page 192

baked beans & sweet potatoes
Prepare the basic recipe, adding 1 peeled and chopped, large sweet potato 1 hour before the end of the cooking time.

baked beans with meatballs
Prepare the basic recipe. Make 2.5-cm (1-in) meatballs from lean minced beef, lamb or pork (page 208). Add the cooked meatballs to the baked beans just before serving.

spicy baked beans
Prepare the basic recipe, adding ½ teaspoon chilli powder.

baked beans with sweet potatoes & cheese
Prepare the basic recipe. Place 2 small sweet potatoes into the oven alongside the casserole 90 minutes before the end of the cooking time. Slice the potatoes in half, pour the beans over them and serve with grated Cheddar cheese sprinkled over the top.

variations

cauliflower cheese

see base recipe page 194

cauliflower cheese with restuffed potato
Prepare the basic recipe, while baking 1 potato. When the potato is cooked, halve, scoop the flesh from the skin and mash with a little butter. Replace the mashed potato in the skin and serve with the cauliflower piled on top. For younger children, just mash the potato with a little cauliflower.

cauliflower cheese with mashed sweet potato
Prepare the basic recipe, adding 1 peeled and chopped sweet potato to the steamer with the cauliflower. Once you remove the cauliflower, let the potato steam another 10 minutes. Purée or mash the sweet potato and serve alongside the baked cauliflower, or mash the potato with the cauliflower for younger children.

cauliflower, leek & cheese bake
Prepare the basic recipe, adding 1 washed and chopped leek (white portion) to the steamer with the cauliflower.

cauliflower, leek, carrot & cheese bake
Prepare the basic recipe, adding 2 chopped carrots and 1 chopped leek (white portion) to the steamer with the cauliflower.

variations

family fish pie

see base recipe page 197

fish & salmon pie
Prepare the basic recipe, replacing the white fish with salmon fillet.

fish pie with peas and broccoli
Prepare the basic recipe, adding 50 g (2 oz) frozen peas and 6–8 broccoli florets to the fish in the casserole dish before you add the cheese sauce.

fish pie with cauliflower
Prepare the basic recipe, adding 6–8 cauliflower florets to the fish in the casserole dish before you add the cheese sauce.

fish pie with carrot & sweet potato topping
Prepare the basic recipe, replacing the potatoes with sweet potatoes.

fish pie with rosti topping
Prepare the basic recipe, omitting the carrot. Instead of chopping and boiling the potatoes, wash, peel and halve them. Boil for 5 minutes, then drain and coarsely grate them over the fish and sauce in the casserole dish. Top with knobs of butter and the grated cheese before baking.

variations

fish fingers

see base recipe page 198

fish fingers with parmesan
Prepare the basic recipe, adding 100 g (4 oz) finely grated Parmesan to the breadcrumbs.

fish fingers with oats
Prepare the basic recipe, replacing the breadcrumbs with 150 g (5 oz) quick-cooking porridge oats.

batter-fried fish fingers
Prepare the basic recipe, omitting the breadcrumbs. Mix the flour and egg together to form a batter. Carefully dip each fish finger into the batter to coat, then cook as before.

fish fingers with crushed chips
Prepare the basic recipe, replacing the breadcrumbs with crushed unsalted potato chips.

variations

moroccan chicken with couscous

see base recipe page 201

moroccan lamb
Prepare the basic recipe, replacing the chicken breasts with 275 g (10 oz) lean lamb leg steak, chopped.

moroccan vegetables
Prepare the basic recipe, replacing the chicken breasts with 225 g (8 oz) tinned chickpeas, drained and rinsed; 1 courgette, washed and chopped; and an extra carrot, washed, peeled and chopped. Replace chicken stock with vegetable stock.

moroccan chicken with raisins
Prepare the basic recipe, replacing the dried apricots with 2 tablespoons chopped raisins.

moroccan beans
Prepare the basic recipe, replacing the chicken with 225 g (8 oz) tinned butter beans, drained and rinsed, and 225 g (8 oz) tinned borlotti beans, drained and rinsed. Replace chicken stock with vegetable stock.

variations

sweet & sour chicken with rice

see base recipe page 202

sweet & sour chicken with noodles
Prepare basic recipe, replacing the rice with 1 nest of egg noodles per person or half a nest (25 g/1 oz) for baby.

sweet & sour pork with rice
Prepare basic recipe, replacing the chicken with 300 g (11 oz) pork tenderloin, chopped.

sweet & sour meatballs with rice
Prepare basic recipe, replacing the chicken with cooked meatballs (page 208).

sweet & sour white fish with rice
Prepare basic recipe, replacing the chicken with 300 g (11 oz) white fish fillet, such as cod, flounder or halibut. Be sure the skin and all bones are removed. Cook 8–10 minutes.

spicy sweet & sour chicken with rice
Prepare basic recipe, adding 1–2 teaspoons sweet chilli sauce to the recipe with the soy sauce.

variations

shepherd's pie

see base recipe page 204

cottage pie
Prepare the basic recipe, replacing the minced lamb with minced beef.

vegetable pie
Prepare the basic recipe, replacing the minced lamb with another peeled and finely chopped carrot, 1 finely chopped courgette and 350–450 g (¾–1 lb) texturized protein (TVP). Replace the stock with 450 g (1 lb) tinned chopped tomatoes.

bean & lentil "shepherd's pie"
Prepare the basic recipe, replacing the minced lamb with 225 g (8 oz) cannellini or borlotti beans and 100 g (4 oz) dried red lentils. Replace the stock with 450 g (1 lb) tinned chopped tomatoes.

shepherd's pie with leek & potato topping
Prepare the basic recipe, replacing 1 large potato with 1 leek (white portion), washed and finely chopped. Steam the leek over the potatoes for the last 10 minutes of cooking. Sprinkled it on the meat before adding the potatoes.

shepherd's pie with sweet potato topping
Prepare the basic recipe, replacing the potatoes with sweet potatoes.

variations

lasagne

see base recipe page 207

spaghetti bolognese
Instead of the basic recipe, make the meat sauce and use it with spaghetti.

lasagne with turkey & cheese sauce
Prepare the basic recipe, replacing the carrot with a few more mushrooms and the minced beef with minced turkey. Replace the tomatoes, tomato paste and stock with another quantity of cheese sauce. Thin down one portion of cheese sauce with an additional 225 ml (8 fl. oz) milk. Layer and bake as before with the thicker sauce on the top.

vegetable lasagne
Prepare the basic recipe, replacing the minced beef with 1 chopped aubergine and 1 chopped courgette, and adding another chopped pepper. Preheat the oven to 200°C (400°F/Gas mark 6). Lay the chopped aubergine, courgette and pepper on a baking tray, drizzle with olive oil and roast for 20 minutes. Transfer to the saucepan, replace the beef stock with vegetable stock, and add 1 teaspoon each chopped fresh oregano and fresh basil. Cook as before.

lentil & mushroom lasagne
Prepare the basic recipe, replacing the minced beef with 125 g (4½ oz) red lentils and doubling the amount of mushrooms. Replace the beef stock with vegetable stock, and cook as before.

variations

beef meatballs

see base recipe page 208

pork & beef meatballs
Prepare the basic recipe, replacing half the minced beef with lean minced pork.

turkey meatballs
Prepare the basic recipe, replacing the minced beef with minced turkey.

lamb meatballs
Prepare the basic recipe, replacing the minced beef with lean minced lamb.

spicy meatballs
Prepare the basic recipe, adding ½ teaspoon ground cumin, ½ teaspoon ground coriander and a pinch of cinnamon with the salt and pepper.

beef & carrot meatballs
Prepare the basic recipe, adding 1 small washed, peeled and finely grated carrot.

variations

pizza

see base recipe page 211

calzone
Prepare the basic recipe, rolling out the dough into 4 circles. Spread a spoonful of tomato sauce on half of each circle, sprinkle with basil leaves and fold over the other half. Press the edges together, sprinkle with mozzarella and bake at 220°C (425°F/Gas mark 7) for 15–20 minutes, until golden brown.

spinach calzone
Prepare the calzone variation above, but replace the basil with 50 g (2 oz) chopped baby spinach. Sprinkle 50 g (2 oz) grated mozzarella on top of the spinach before folding over the other half of dough. Press the edges of the calzone together, brush with beaten egg, and bake at 220°C (425°F/Gas mark 7) for 15–20 minutes, until golden brown.

pizza swirls
Prepare the basic dough recipe, and split the dough into 6–8 pieces. Stretch each piece into a sausage shape, then flatten. Spread sun-dried tomato paste along the flattened side and roll up. Lay the swirls on their side, next to each other, in a greased deep cake tin, with a little space between them. Cover with clingfilm and leave in a warm place for 30 minutes until they have doubled in size. Bake at 220°C (425°F/Gas mark 7) for 10–15 minutes, until golden brown.

variations

mini quiches

see base recipe page 212

salmon mini quiches
Prepare the basic recipe, adding 75 g (3 oz) chopped cooked salmon to the crust before filling with the egg and milk mixture.

broccoli mini quiches
Prepare the basic recipe, adding 75 g (3 oz) cooked broccoli florets to the crust before filling with the egg and milk mixture.

spinach & cheese mini quiches
Prepare the basic recipe, adding 75 g (3 oz) torn spinach leaves to the crust before filling with the egg and milk mixture, and replacing the Cheddar cheese with 50 g (2 oz) crumbled pasteurized feta cheese. Do not use unpasteurized feta for children under 3 years old.

mini quiche lorraine
Prepare the basic recipe, adding 75 g (3 oz) chopped cooked ham or bacon to the crust before filling with the egg and milk mixture.

mushroom & tomato mini quiches
Prepare the basic recipe, adding 50 g (2 oz) chopped mushrooms and 4 skinned, chopped tomatoes to the crust before filling with the egg and milk mixture.

focaccia

see base recipe page 215

sun-dried tomato focaccia
Prepare the basic recipe, adding 3 chopped sun-dried tomatoes to the recipe.

olive focaccia
Prepare the basic recipe, adding 6–8 finely chopped pitted green olives to
the recipe.

garlic focaccia
Prepare the basic recipe, replacing the olive oil for drizzling with garlic oil. To
make it, very finely chop 1 garlic clove, then pound it with 1 tablespoon olive
oil in a mortar with a pestle. Strain, then drizzle over the focaccia just prior
to baking.

mozzarella focaccia
Prepare the basic recipe. Before baking the focaccia, drain, then tear a ball of
fresh mozzarella cheese into small pieces. Place the cheese pieces in the
indentations in the top of the dough.

cherry tomato focaccia
Prepare the basic recipe. Before baking the focaccia, quarter 10 cherry tomatoes
and place them in the indentations in the top of the dough.

variations

cheese biscuits

see base recipe page 216

cheese-biscuit pizzas
Prepare the basic recipe, but split the dough into four equal parts. With
a rolling pin, roll each part into a flat circle, top with pizza sauce and the
pizza toppings of your choice, sprinkle with mozzarella cheese, and bake
for 15–20 minutes, until the cheese has melted and the crust is golden
brown and crispy.

plain biscuits
Prepare the basic recipe, omitting the cheese in the base.

cheesy fingers
Prepare the basic recipe. Split the dough into 10 pieces, roll each one into a
ball, then flatten and shape into 'fingers'. Sprinkle each one with a little
grated Parmesan and bake for 5–10 minutes.

cheese & sun-dried tomato biscuits
Prepare the basic recipe, adding 1 tablespoon sun-dried tomato paste or
5–6 finely chopped sun-dried tomatoes at the same time as the Cheddar.

variations

savoury cheese muffins

see base recipe page 217

savoury cheese muffins with sun-dried tomato
Prepare the basic recipe, adding 2 tablespoons sun-dried tomato paste to the mixture when you add the egg, milk, and melted butter.

savoury olive muffins
Prepare the basic recipe, replacing the cheese with 2 tablespoons finely chopped black or green olives.

savoury muffins with pesto & pine nuts
Prepare the basic recipe, replacing the cheese with 2 tablespoons pesto and 100 g (4 oz) pine nuts.

savoury muffins with pesto & parmesan cheese
Prepare the basic recipe, replacing the cheese with 2 tablespoons pesto and 2 tablespoons grated Parmesan cheese. Sprinkle a few pine nuts over the top of the muffins before baking.

savoury muffins with tapenade
Prepare the basic recipe, replacing the cheese with 2 tablespoons tapenade in any flavour.

variations

soda bread

see base recipe page 218

soda bread with cheese
Prepare the basic recipe, adding 175 g (6 oz) grated hard cheese to the dry ingredients. Grate a little cheese on top of each bread just before baking.

soda bread with cheese & chives
Prepare the basic recipe, adding 175 g (6 oz) grated hard cheese and chopped fresh chives. Grate a little cheese on top of each bread just before baking.

soda bread with sun-dried tomatoes
Prepare the basic recipe, adding 50 g (2 oz) drained and chopped sun-dried tomatoes with the dry ingredients.

soda bread with sun-dried tomatoes & olives
Prepare the basic recipe, adding 50 g (2 oz) drained and chopped sun-dried tomatoes and 50 g (2 oz) chopped olives with the dry ingredients.

soda bread with sun-dried tomatoes, cheese & seeds
Prepare the basic recipe, adding 50 g (2 oz) drained and chopped sun-dried tomatoes, 175 g (6 oz) grated Parmesan cheese, and 3 tablespoons sunflower or pumpkin seeds with the dry ingredients. Grate a little cheese on top of each soda bread and sprinkle with a few seeds just before baking.

cheddar palmiers

see base recipe page 221

cheese straws
Prepare the basic recipe, but sprinkle all the cheese over half of the pastry, fold over, roll out again, and cut into 1-cm (½-in) wide strips.

sweet cinnamon palmiers
Prepare the basic recipe, replacing the cheese with 1 teaspoon sugar mixed with ½ teaspoon ground cinnamon.

pesto palmiers
Prepare the basic recipe, replacing the cheese with 1 tablespoon pesto. Spread ⅔ of the pesto on the pastry and the remaining ⅓ on the rolled-up section as for the cheese version.

cheese & sun-dried tomato palmiers
Prepare the basic recipe, spreading 1 tablespoon sun-dried tomato paste on the pastry before sprinkling on the cheese.

variations

griddle scones

see base recipe page 222

savoury cheese griddle scones
Prepare the basic recipe, omitting the sugar and replacing it with 25 g (1 oz) finely grated Parmesan or another hard cheese.

orange griddle scones
Prepare the basic recipe, adding the grated zest and juice of 1 orange and reducing the amount of milk slightly.

raisin griddle scones
Prepare the basic recipe, adding 1 heaping tablespoon raisins with the flour.

apricot griddle scones
Prepare the basic recipe, adding 4–5 chopped, dried apricots with the flour. If you want to give these to a younger baby, chop the apricots very finely and omit the sugar.

chocolate chip griddle scones
Prepare the basic recipe. Once you turn over the griddle scones, sprinkle 4–5 dark chocolate chips onto each one. The chocolate will melt while the griddle scones finish cooking. Serve warm.

oaty biscuits

see base recipe page 225

oaty biscuits with sunflower seeds
Prepare the basic recipe, adding 1 tablespoon sunflower seeds to the
dry ingredients.

oaty biscuits with pumpkin seeds
Prepare the basic recipe, adding 1 tablespoon pumpkin seeds to the
dry ingredients.

oaty biscuits with currants
Prepare the basic recipe, replacing the raisins with currants.

oaty biscuits with orange
Prepare the basic recipe, adding the finely grated zest of 2 oranges to the dry
ingredients and omitting the nutmeg.

oaty biscuits with chopped hazelnuts
Prepare the basic recipe, using half the amount of raisins and the same amount
of chopped hazelnuts. These are not suitable for children and adults with
nut allergies.

variations

fruit muffins

see base recipe page 226

banana muffins
Prepare the basic recipe, replacing the berries with 3 peeled and mashed ripe bananas and 1 teaspoon ground cinnamon.

pear & ginger muffins
Prepare the basic recipe, replacing the berries with 3 peeled, cored and chopped ripe pears and 1 teaspoon ground ginger.

apple–raisin muffins
Prepare the basic recipe, replacing the berries with 2 peeled, cored and grated apples, and 50 g (2 oz) raisins.

wholemeal apple–apricot muffins
Prepare the basic recipe, replacing the self-raising flour with 100 g (4 oz) wholemeal flour and an additional 1 teaspoon baking powder. Also, replace the berries with 2 peeled, cored and grated apples and 75 g (3 oz) chopped dried or fresh peeled apricots.

peach–raspberry muffins
Prepare the basic recipe, replacing the berries with 2 peeled, pitted and finely chopped peaches and 2 tablespoons raspberries.

variations

gingerbread men

see base recipe page 229

'cinnamen'
Prepare the basic recipe, replacing the ground ginger with 1½ teaspoons ground cinnamon.

gingerbread men with mixed spices
Prepare the basic recipe, adding 1 teaspoon ground cinnamon and ½ teaspoon ground cloves to the mixture.

glazed gingerbread men
Prepare the basic recipe. When the gingerbread men have cooled, mix up a thin icing using icing sugar and freshly squeezed lemon juice. Put the gingerbread men on a cooling rack set over some parchment or wax paper, and drizzle the icing over them. The paper will catch the drips of icing and help reduce the amount of clearing up.

gingerbread and raisin biscuits
Prepare the basic recipe, stirring 100 g (4 oz) of raisins into the gingerbread mixture. Instead of gingerbread men shapes, make biscuits using a biscuit cutter.

variations

thumbprint cookies

see base recipe page 230

plain cookies
Prepare the basic recipe, omitting the raspberry jam. You can make these for 9-month-old babies, if they've already had some solid foods, as long as you use breast milk or formula instead of cow's milk.

currant cookies
Prepare the basic recipe, adding 75 g (3 oz) currants at the same time as the flour and omitting the raspberry jam.

orange cookies
Prepare the basic recipe, adding the finely grated zest of 1 orange to the dough and replacing the raspberry jam with orange curd.

apple–raisin cookies
Prepare the basic recipe, adding 1 peeled, cored, and grated apple and 75 g (3 oz) raisins at the same time as the flour. Omit the raspberry jam.

variations

pineapple kebabs with yoghurt

see base recipe page 233

pineapple & banana kebabs with yoghurt
Prepare the basic recipe, replacing half the pineapple with 2 bananas, peeled and chopped into chunks. Alternate the banana with the pineapple on the skewers.

pineapple & strawberry kebabs with yoghurt
Prepare the basic recipe, replacing half the pineapple with 100 g (4 oz) strawberries, hulled and chopped into chunks. Alternate the strawberries with the pineapple on the skewers.

mixed fruit kebabs with yoghurt
Prepare the basic recipe, replacing half the pineapple with 1 banana and 1 mango, peeled and chopped into chunks, and 4 strawberries, chopped into chunks. Alternate the different fruit on the skewers.

pineapple kebabs with raspberry & yoghurt
Prepare the basic recipe. Mash 50 g (2 oz) raspberries and strain to remove the seeds. Swirl into the yoghurt dip.

variations

peach cobbler

see base recipe page 234

apple & raspberry cobbler
Prepare the basic recipe, replacing the peaches with 4 apples, washed,
peeled, cored and chopped, and 100 g (4 oz) raspberries.

pear cobbler
Prepare the basic recipe, replacing the peaches with 4 ripe pears, washed,
peeled, cored and chopped.

blueberry cobbler
Prepare the basic recipe, replacing the peaches with 400 g (14 oz) fresh or
thawed frozen blueberries.

rhubarb cobbler
Prepare the basic recipe, omitting the lemon juice and replacing the peaches
with 400 g (14 oz) chopped fresh rhubarb.

chocolate ice cream

see base recipe page 237

mint chocolate ice cream
Prepare the basic recipe, adding 2 teaspoons peppermint extract. If you want your ice cream to be green, add a little green food colouring.

white chocolate ice cream
Prepare the basic recipe, replacing the dark chocolate chips with 480 g (1 lb) melted white chocolate before transferring the churned ice cream to the freezer to solidify.

chocolate chip ice cream
Prepare the basic recipe. Instead of melting the chocolate chips before adding to the mixture, add 180 g (6 oz) white chocolate chips and 180 g (6 oz) milk chocolate chips to the mixture when you start to churn.

toffee ice cream
Prepare the basic recipe, adding 160 g (5 ½ oz) chopped fudge or soft toffee pieces when you start to churn.

strawberry ice cream
Prepare the basic recipe, adding 150 g (5 oz) chopped fresh strawberries when you start to churn.

variations

côpote

see base recipe page 238

rhubarb & ginger côpote
Prepare the basic recipe, replacing the dried fruit with 450 g (1 lb) rhubarb, cut into 1-cm (½-in) pieces, and adding 175 g (6 oz) brown sugar. Replace the cloves with ½ teaspoon ground ginger.

ice cream compôte ripple
Prepare the basic recipe, purée the compôte, cool, then swirl through slightly softened vanilla ice cream to serve.

apple & apricot compôte
Prepare the basic recipe, replacing the dried fruit with 225 g (8oz) dried apricots and 3 fresh apples, washed, peeled, cored and chopped.

apple, pear & plum compôte
Prepare the basic recipe, replacing the dried fruit with 1 apple and 1 pear, washed, peeled, cored and chopped, and 3 plums, peeled, pitted and chopped.

mixed berry compôte
Prepare the basic recipe, replacing the dried fruit with 200 g (7 oz) raspberries, 200 g (7 oz) blueberries, and 200 g (7 oz) hulled and chopped strawberries. Replace the juice with 100 ml (4 fl. oz) water.

variations

rhubarb fool

see base recipe page 240

blueberry fool
Prepare the basic recipe, replacing the rhubarb with 200 g (7 oz) fresh or thawed frozen blueberries.

apple & cinnamon fool
Prepare the basic recipe, replacing the rhubarb with 3 washed, peeled, cored and chopped apples and ½ teaspoon ground cinnamon.

banana & orange fool
Prepare the basic recipe, replacing the rhubarb with 2 mashed bananas and the zest and juice of 1 orange. Omit the cooking step. Just mix by hand.

berry fool
Prepare the basic recipe, replacing the rhubarb with 200 g (7 oz) of your favourite fresh or thawed frozen berries.

index